# Regional Aspects of
# Canada's Economic Growth

# CANADIAN STUDIES IN ECONOMICS

A series of studies now edited by Douglas G. Hartle, sponsored by the Social Science Research Council of Canada, and published with financial assistance from the Canada Council.

ALAN G. GREEN

# Regional Aspects of
# Canada's Economic Growth

University of Toronto Press

© University of Toronto Press 1971
Printed in the Netherlands for
University of Toronto Press, Toronto and Buffalo
ISBN 0-8020-1629-4

# Preface

REGIONAL DISPARITIES in income have been an important part of the growth experience of most nation states. Canada is no exception. In a large country, thinly populated and having a wide diversity of resources, cultures, and locational advantages, it is only natural to expect the existence of dissimilar levels of economic performance. In fact, just this diversity of physical and human backgrounds has often provided the primary thrust for variations in national economic growth. If, therefore, a better understanding of national development is to be obtained, some attention to the growth experience of the subnational units is imperative. This study aims at widening our understanding of the Canadian growth process by focusing on the relationship between regional and national changes since the last decade of the nineteenth century.

Two different approaches are used in the discussion of regional income inequality. The first (carried out in chapter one) is a cross-section analysis; the year chosen was 1956. This approach provides an opportunity to study, in some detail, the main causes of observed regional income disparity and simultaneously to compare these regional differences with observed international differences. This chapter seeks answers to questions concerning the importance of provincial differences in labour force participation ratios, structural differences in output, and intersectoral variations in relative output per worker.

With this background to recent regional inequalities, the emphasis shifts to long-term changes in regional growth. This is accomplished by measuring regional levels of gross value added at four points of time: 1890-91, 1910-11, 1929, and 1956. Such a perspective provides an opportunity to pursue a fairly intensive investigation into the trends in regional income inequality. It also provides an opportunity to observe variations, through time, in the regional structure of production, an essential part of any study which seeks to relate regional and national development through an investigation of changes in regional participation. This long-term segment is carried out in chapters two and three, and the results of the statistical study are brought together in chapter four.

The primary purpose of this study is to develop a first set of regional income (here, gross value added) estimates in order to give some perspective to the historical growth experience of Canadian regions, to see, with this data, if some pattern between regional and national development can be discerned, and in particular to study the role played by these subnational units in promoting or retarding national growth.

This monograph was written as my doctoral dissertation at Harvard University under the direction of Professor Simon Kuznets, whose suggestions, encouragement, and constant interest in this project were invaluable at all stages. Professor Caves of Harvard also offered some suggestions for improving the original manuscript.

Two specific appointments were invaluable to the final completion of the project: the first as a Fellow of the Institute for Economic Research at Queen's University during the summer of 1965; the second, also granted by Queen's University, as a R. Samuel McLaughlin Research Fellow in Economics during the academic year 1967-68. This assistance is gratefully acknowledged. This work has been published with the help of a grant from the Social Science Research Council of Canada using funds provided by the Canada Council.

Part of the material of chapter two has been published in an article entitled "Regional Aspects of Canada's Economic Growth, 1890-1929" in *Canadian Journal of Economics and Political Science*, vol. XXXIII (May 1967), 232-45.

Finally, the debt any author owes to his family and particularly his wife is always great. In this case the encouragement and assistance provided by my wife Ann went beyond all call of duty and although a simple thank you is necessary, it is a long way from the tribute she deserves.

A.G.G.

# Contents

# Tables

# 1
# Provincial Differences in Income, Output, and Labour Force for 1956

THIS CHAPTER will consist of a discussion of the factors contributing to inter-regional income inequality as observed in 1956. The following questions will be considered: How large are regional income differences in 1956 and how do these compare with international inequalities? What influence do property, service, and transfer incomes have on the observed total income differential? What impact do differences in the age-sex composition and quality of the labour force exert on inequality? What is the relationship between the level of income per capita and the industrial structure of a region? What role do intersectoral versus intrasectoral differences play in explaining regional income differences?

The answers to these questions will help determine why, in an advanced stage of national development, interregional income differences still exist. Indirectly, such an investigation points up the net effects of all the long-term influences that have acted on the regions. In addition, the cross-section study will serve as a backdrop to the long-term trends outlined in succeeding chapters.

UNITS AND INCOME TOTALS DEFINED

The area units used throughout this study are the provinces. Newfoundland and the Northwest Territories are excluded because of scarcity of data, and, in the case of Newfoundland, because of its short history as a full member of the Dominion. A main consideration in choosing provincial units is that they will lend continuity to this analysis. Another important criterion is the degree of autonomous control each province exerts over its own development as outlined in the British North America Act of 1867, which gives to each province exclusive control over such matters as direct taxation within the province, incorporation of companies with provincial objectives, education (subject to certain restrictions relating to the establishment of schools by religious minorities), and the management and sale of public lands and of timber and other resources thereon. This last point is especially important, because Canada has developed primarily through the export of such resources.

TABLE I-1

Land area, population, and population density of Canada and its Provinces, 1951

| Provinces | Land area Square miles (thousands) | Per cent | Population Number (thousands) | Per cent | Density |
|---|---|---|---|---|---|
| | (1) | (2) | (3) | (4) | (5) |
| 1. P.E.I.* | 2 | 0.11 | 98 | 0.72 | 45.07 |
| 2. Nova Scotia | 21 | 1.04 | 642 | 4.72 | 30.98 |
| 3. New Brunswick | 27 | 1.37 | 515 | 3.79 | 18.77 |
| 4. Quebec | 524 | 26.15 | 4,055 | 29.79 | 7.74 |
| 5. Ontario | 363 | 18.13 | 4,597 | 33.77 | 12.66 |
| 6. Manitoba | 220 | 10.91 | 776 | 5.70 | 3.53 |
| 7. Saskatchewan | 238 | 11.88 | 831 | 6.11 | 3.50 |
| 8. Alberta | 249 | 12.42 | 939 | 6.90 | 3.78 |
| 9. British Columbia | 359 | 17.93 | 1,165 | 8.56 | 3.24 |
| 10. Canada | 2,003 | 100.00 | 13,612 | 100.00 | |

* Prince Edward Island.

SOURCE:   *Census of Canada, 1951,* vol. I, 2.

Table I-1 presents provincial differences in land area, size of population, and population density. The first observation to be drawn from the table is the dominance of Ontario and Quebec in both land area and population. The second is the sharp difference in population density between the maritime provinces (Prince Edward Island, Nova Scotia, and New Brunswick) in the east, and the prairie provinces (Manitoba, Saskatchewan, and Alberta) and British Columbia in the west. The former are characterized by a relatively small share of the land area but with fairly dense population, while the latter exhibit the opposite characteristics. Ontario and Quebec fall midway between these extremes. Another interesting point, although not shown in this table, is that approximately 75 per cent of the total population resides within two hundred miles of the Canadian-American border.[1] Besides these space and population differences the provinces differ widely in natural resource endowment, an important factor in Canadian regional development.

The decision to use provincial area units dictates that personal income totals be employed in measuring the economic position of the provinces, because national income data are not distributed geographically. However, the difference between these two totals in 1956 was only 5 per cent representing, in the main, undistributed corporate profits.[2] The exclusion of these items should not alter the relative income position of the provinces.

Total personal income represents the sum of wages and salaries, proprietors' incomes (which also include the return on capital invested—this latter source of revenue is difficult to separate), and transfer income (e.g., government transfer payments such as unemployment insurance and old age pension payments); this total does not include interest on the public debt, which is classified under property income. Theoretically, it is possible to divide these totals (except for transfer income which does not arise from productive activity) by industrial origin by province. In Canada, however, the only breakdown by industrial origin on a provincial basis is between the two broad categories of agricultural and non-agricultural income, and this is only for service income (the total of wages and salaries and proprietors' incomes). This limits our use of personal income, and in particular service income, in explaining the total per capita income differentials observed. A more detailed analysis of these relative income levels must be made, then, in terms of other economic variables such as the industrial distribution of output (gross value added) and the distribution of the labour force by industry, and in terms of certain demographic variables such as the age and sex structure of the province's population and labour force.

Personal income in this study appears in current dollar totals. The effect of this is to reduce the meaningfulness of interprovincial comparisons because of the possible occurrence of differential variations between income and price levels among the provinces. For example, if in a low income province the cost of living is lower than in a high income province, measured in terms of a uniform basket of good, then part of the money income differential observed is automatically absorbed. The result is that the true interprovincial difference is overestimated. Conversely, it is possible, although not likely, for income and prices to vary inversely, in which case the current price totals understate the provincial difference.

Another indication of the bias in income differentials may be provided by a comparison between urban and rural prices. In a study, "Farm and Urban Purchasing Power," Nathan Koffsky compared two budgets, farm and urban (for a comparable basket of goods), for 1941.[3] Both were evaluated in terms of prices paid on the farm and prices paid in urban communities, and the comparison was made for the nation as a whole. Koffsky found that the farm budget would be 30 per cent more in terms of urban prices (the greatest difference occurring in food costs). If the results of this study are fairly accurate (and his estimates are probably generous), it would mean that a comparison of agriculture and non-agriculture service incomes in current dollars would overestimate the difference between these two levels.

This same factor also affects our interprovincial comparisons. If we assume one area unit to be completely urbanized and another to be completely rural and the current dollar income range to be 2 to 1 in favour of the former, then by applying Koffsky's findings to the farm area unit's income, the range would be reduced by approximately one-half (to about 1.5 to 1). Thus, the results outlined in the subsequent sections regarding differences in the level of personal income between regions and between sectors (agriculture versus non-agriculture) must be tempered by the implications of the use of money instead of real income values.

PROVINCIAL DIFFERENCES IN PER CAPITA INCOME

In the light of the large differences in the size of the units, the balance of the discussion on the differences in income levels between provinces and the possible causes of such disparities will be presented in the form of weighted averages. This weighting procedure, it is hoped, will reduce the biases inherent in treating Ontario and Quebec as equal partners with the other seven provinces.

Table I-2 presents both the unweighted differences in per capita income and a weighted measure of income inequality (weighted by the share of each province in total population). To obtain the latter, the population shares (col 4) were subtracted from the income shares (col 2), and the resulting differences were totalled, disregarding signs (line 10, col 7). For such a measure, the possible range of the total deviation (as in a two-region economy) would be 200 (where one region had all the income and the other all the population) to zero (where both regions shared equally in population and income). In the subsequent discussion as we break down this aggregate income measure into its components and measure the resulting weighted disparities, any movement which reduces the total deviation implies a reduction in interregional income inequalities.

The first conclusion to be drawn from the data in Table I-2 is that the range in per capita incomes is approximately 2 to 1.[4] This result is vastly different from that observed when international per capita income differences are calculated, that differential approximating 15 to 1.[5] The Canadian interregional differentials are closer to those found in the United States, where the range between states for 1955 was found to be 2 to 1.[6] These lower intranational ranges in Canada and the United States are due to a greater degree of internal factor mobility than to such international flows, and to the pressure placed on the federal governments to eliminate regional income differences. In the case of international disparities, no such authority exists.

Turning now to the weighted measure of income inequality (col 7), we note two important results. The first is that Ontario and Quebec account for almost two-thirds (10.4) of the total disparity, and that signs of their deviations between population and income are different. Secondly, the balance of the provinces is apparently split into two groups: the maritime provinces with negative deviations, and the western provinces (Manitoba excepted) with positive deviations, or per capita income levels greater than the national average. The overall result is that the provinces are divided into two contrasting groups: Ontario and Quebec, both large and both accounting for a significant amount of the total disparity; and the maritime and western provinces, smaller than Ontario and Quebec and accounting for the remaining differences.

PROVINCIAL DIFFERENCES IN SERVICE, PROPERTY,
AND TRANSFER INCOME PER CAPITA

The next step in analysing the differences in provincial income levels is to dis-

## TABLE I-2

Sum (disregarding signs) of deviations of shares of population from shares of personal income (current dollars), and unweighted relative per capita income for provinces, 1956

| Provinces in declining order of per capita personal income | Personal income | | Population | | Personal income per capita | Per capita income relative to unweighted countrywide mean | Deviations from population shares of personal income shares |
| | Millions of current $ | Per cent | Thousands | Per cent | | | |
| | (1) | (2) | (3) | (4) | (5) | (6) | (7) |
| 1. British Columbia | 2,332 | 10.8 | 1,399 | 8.9 | 1,667 | 133.57 | +1.9 |
| 2. Ontario | 8,617 | 40.1 | 5,405 | 34.6 | 1,594 | 127.72 | +5.5 |
| 3. Alberta | 1,635 | 7.6 | 1,123 | 7.2 | 1,456 | 116.67 | +0.4 |
| 4. Saskatchewan | 1,226 | 5.7 | 881 | 5.6 | 1,392 | 111.54 | +0.1 |
| 5. Manitoba | 1,126 | 5.2 | 850 | 5.4 | 1,325 | 106.17 | −0.2 |
| 6. Quebec | 5,318 | 24.7 | 4,628 | 29.6 | 1,149 | 92.07 | −4.9 |
| 7. Nova Scotia | 675 | 3.1 | 695 | 4.4 | 971 | 77.80 | −1.3 |
| 8. New Brunswick | 497 | 2.3 | 555 | 3.5 | 895 | 71.71 | −1.2 |
| 9. P.E.I. | 78 | 0.4 | 99 | 0.6 | 788 | 63.14 | −0.2 |
| 10. Total | 21,504 | 100.0 | 15,635 | 100.0 | | | 15.7 |
| 11. Unweighted mean 1 to 9 | | | | | 1,248 | | |
| 12. Range 1 to 9 | | | | | 2.1 | | |

SOURCE AND METHOD: Col 1: *National Accounts Income and Expenditure, 1960*, 40; col 3: *Ibid.*, p. 60; col. 5: col 1 divided by col 3; col 6: rows 1 to 9 of col 5 divided, respectively, by $1,248; col 7: col 2 less col 4; line 10, col 7: sum, disregarding signs.

aggregate total personal income into its three main components–service, property, and transfer income–in order to study the behaviour of these three income groups at various levels of provincial per capita income. Columns 7, 8, and 9 of Table I-3 were constructed in the same way as column 7 of Table I-2 and show, as did the latter, the weighted inequality, in per capita terms, of the three income groups. From Table I-3 we note that the behaviour of the two contrasting groups outlined in the previous section persists here in service and property incomes but is modified somewhat in the case of transfer income, for which British Columbia is the dominant contributor to total inequality. Further, both service and property incomes show greater totals (line 10, cols 7 and 8) than total personal income, while transfer income is smaller.

Two implications arise from these findings. First, the same change in the weighted inequality observed when property and transfer incomes were eliminated shows that inequality in service income per capita between the provinces is the major cause of inequality in total income. Second, the smaller total deviation for transfer income and the differences in sign between column 9 on the one hand and columns 7 and 8 on the other suggest that transfer income tends to reduce overall inequality. To check if, indeed, the latter is the case, the weighted inequalities (line 10, cols 7, 8, and 9) were multiplied by their weights in the aggregate (line 10, cols 10, 11, and 12), and the results (line 11, cols 7, 8, and 9) were totalled. The sum of these three figures yielded a total of 16.2, which is greater than the original total inequality found in Table I-2 (15.7). From this we can infer that some cancellation among the three types of income with respect to their interprovincial differences occurs, that is, transfer incomes reduce interprovincial differences in per capita incomes, but only slightly. Conversely, we expect service and property incomes to be positively associated with levels of total per capita income.[7] In the case of the service income the positive association occurs because it represents the largest (4/5) component of total personal income (col 10), and because higher levels of income are partially the effect of these high levels of wages, salaries, and proprietors' incomes. That this is the case can be seen in column 7, which shows that the four provinces with the highest per capita incomes all have positive signs for the deviations between service income and population shares. Property income is also positively associated with a rising level of per capita income (col 8). Here, however, the reason is less clear. It may be that the higher income provinces are able to save more out of current income than the poorer areas, and also offer greater incentives to foreign lenders. The effects are cumulative, so that as investment increases so does income. Thus, the high income provinces gain increasing amounts of revenue from property income, enhancing their position relative to the lower income provinces.

Transfer incomes do appear to offset the effects of these other two forms of income, but again only slightly. For example, column 9 shows a mixed pattern of signs for deviations from population shares of transfer income shares. In fact,

# TABLE I-3

Sum (disregarding signs) of deviations from shares of population of shares of service, property, and transfer income (current dollars) for provinces, 1956

| Provinces in declining order of per capita income | Service income | | Property income | | Transfer income | | Deviation from population shares of | | | Share of components in total personal income | | |
|---|---|---|---|---|---|---|---|---|---|---|---|---|
| | Millions of $ | Per cent | Millions of $ | Per cent | Millions of $ | Per cent | Service income shares | Property income shares | Transfer income shares | Service income | Property income | Transfer income |
| | (1) | (2) | (3) | (4) | (5) | (6) | (7) | (8) | (9) | (10) | (11) | (12) |
| 1. British Columbia | 1,947 | 10.8 | 199 | 10.5 | 224 | 13.0 | +1.9 | +1.6 | +4.1 | 83.5 | 8.5 | 9.6 |
| 2. Ontario | 7,231 | 40.2 | 850 | 45.0 | 549 | 32.0 | +5.6 | +10.4 | -2.6 | 83.9 | 9.9 | 6.4 |
| 3. Alberta | 1,389 | 7.7 | 129 | 6.8 | 121 | 7.0 | +0.5 | -0.4 | -0.2 | 85.0 | 7.9 | 7.4 |
| 4. Saskatchewan | 1,046 | 5.8 | 83 | 4.4 | 105 | 6.1 | +0.2 | -1.2 | +0.5 | 85.3 | 6.8 | 8.6 |
| 5. Manitoba | 936 | 5.2 | 94 | 5.0 | 89 | 5.2 | -0.2 | -0.4 | -0.2 | 83.1 | 8.3 | 7.9 |
| 6. Quebec | 4,442 | 24.7 | 446 | 23.6 | 483 | 28.1 | -4.9 | -6.0 | -1.5 | 83.5 | 8.4 | 9.1 |
| 7. Nova Scotia | 531 | 3.0 | 48 | 2.5 | 73 | 4.3 | -1.4 | -1.9 | -0.1 | 78.7 | 7.1 | 10.8 |
| 8. New Brunswick | 404 | 2.2 | 34 | 1.8 | 62 | 3.6 | -1.3 | -1.7 | +0.1 | 81.3 | 6.8 | 12.5 |
| 9. P.E.I. | 59 | 0.3 | 6 | 0.3 | 11 | 0.6 | -0.3 | -0.3 | 0.0 | 75.6 | 7.7 | 14.1 |
| 10. Total | 17,985 | 100.0 | 1,889 | 100.0 | 1,717 | 100.0 | 16.3 | 23.9 | 9.3 | 82.2 | 7.9 | 9.6 |
| 11. Adjusted disparities | | | | | | | 13.4 | 1.9 | 0.9 | | | |

NOTE: Cols 10, 11, and 12: Shares do not add to 100 since sums of components do not agree with sum of total personal income.

SOURCE AND METHOD: Cols 1, 3, and 5: *National Accounts Income and Expenditure, 1960,* 41-3; col 7: col 2 less col 4 of Table I-2; col 8: col 4 less col 4 of Table I-2; col 9: col 6 less col 4 of Table I-2; line 10, cols 7, 8, and 9: sums disregarding signs; line 11: calculated by multiplying the weighted disparities (line 10) of the three income types by their weights in the aggregate (line 10, cols 10, 11, and 12).

the largest positive deviation is recorded for the highest income province. To explain this apparent anomaly, it is necessary to distinguish intraprovincial transfer payments from interprovincial transfers. The largest single item included in the former, at least for Canada, is the hospital insurance payment. Both Saskatchewan and British Columbia have such a plan, which partly accounts for their positive deviations between shares and implies, abstracting from political considerations, that only the richer provinces are free to indulge in such a welfare scheme–automatically offsetting our expectations of a negative association between transfer income and the total. Similarly, the richer provinces are more likely to receive interprovincial transfer payments than the poorer. For example, British Columbia has been plagued from time to time by above average amounts of unemployment (Table I-4, cols 3 and 4, line 1), with the result that

TABLE I-4

Provincial comparison of unemployment levels and percentage of the population retired, 1951

| Provinces in declining order of per capita income | Per cent retired [a] | | Per cent unemployed [b] | |
|---|---|---|---|---|
| | Male (1) | Female (2) | Male (3) | Female (4) |
| 1. British Columbia | 11.4 | 3.9 | 2.0 | 1.8 |
| 2. Ontario | 5.9 | 3.0 | 0.9 | 0.9 |
| 3. Alberta | 6.9 | 2.7 | 0.8 | 0.9 |
| 4. Saskatchewan | 7.4 | 2.8 | 0.5 | 0.8 |
| 5. Manitoba | 8.2 | 3.3 | 1.1 | 1.1 |
| 6. Quebec | 4.5 | 2.3 | 2.1 | 1.5 |
| 7. Nova Scotia | 7.3 | 3.3 | 2.8 | 1.6 |
| 8. New Brunswick | 6.6 | 3.4 | 2.5 | 1.6 |
| 9. Prince Edward Island | 6.2 | 3.9 | 1.3 | 1.1 |
| 10. Canada (weighted average) | 6.4 | 2.9 | 1.5 | 1.2 |

NOTES:    [a] This is the percentage to population over 14 years.
              [b] This is the percentage of the total labour force.
SOURCE:    *Census of Canada, 1951*, vol. IV, Table 1.

large amounts of unemployment benefits flow to this province. Also, in provinces like Ontario, which are industrialized, a highly organized payment mechanism for unemployment benefits exists. Thus, the majority of the unemployed receive benefits. Also, the unemployment period tends to be relatively short so those out of work receive benefits the total time. Conversely, in the low income, less industrialized provinces, the same opportunity to collect unemployment insurance does not exist because, for example, many of the occupations are not covered under the scheme, and because unemployment is generally more chronic in these areas and benefits tend to run out before work is found. The result, then, is that more transfer payments per capita flow towards the higher income provinces.

Saskatchewan and British Columbia also have other factors operating to increase their receipt of transfer payments. In Saskatchewan a major contribution comes from the federal government in the form of payments under the Prairie Farm Assistance Act; in British Columbia, a large flow of transfer payments is received in the form of old age pensions as a result of the attraction this province has for retired people (cols 1 and 2).

SERVICE INCOME

Service income is the largest single component of total personal income, and it deserves close attention. The first step in analysing the factors causing inequality between provinces in this component is to see how much of this observed inequality is the result of differences in the ratio of labour force to total population among the provinces. Other things being equal, our expectation is that where service income per capita is high the ratio of labour force to population will be high.

To calculate the weighted differences in the ratio of labour force to population, the provincial shares of population were subtracted from the respective shares of the labour force, and the deviations were totalled, disregarding signs (Table I-5, col 3). The data indicate the existence of a weak but positive association between this ratio and differing levels of per capita service income (col 7, Table I-3). We would expect a positive association, because a high labour force to population ratio, all other conditions being equal, is an important reason for a province enjoying a high level of service income per capita. Also, on the effect side, we would expect that a province with a high service income per capita attracts population from lower income areas, especially population of working age, so raising the ratio of labour force to total population.

To estimate the effect of these varying ratios of labour force to total population on the inequality in service income per capita, provincial shares of the labour force were subtracted from the respective shares of service income, and the resulting deviations totalled (signs disregarded). This total (line 10, col. 4) yields a weighted measure of the inequality in service income per capita with the effects of differing ratios of labour force to population eliminated. Comparing the total weighted inequality in service income per worker, 12.3, with the total for service income per capita, 16.3 (Table I-3, col 7, line 10), we note that by standardizing different ratios of labour force in total population the latter inequality has been reduced by approximately a fifth. This demonstrates that differences between provinces in labour force participation rates do play a role in explaining interprovincial inequalities in service income per capita.

Inequality in service income per capita is affected not only by differences in labour force participation rates, but also by differences in the quality of the labour force among regions. The age-sex composition of the labour force is one

# TABLE I-5

Sum (disregarding signs) of deviations from population and service income (current dollars) shares of labour force and male-equivalent labour force shares, for provinces, 1956

| Provinces in declining order of per capita income | Labour force | | Deviation from population shares of labour force shares | Deviation from labour force shares of service income shares | Male-equivalent labour force, 1951 | | Deviation from population shares of Male-equivalent labour force shares | Deviation from Male-equivalent labour force shares of service income shares |
|---|---|---|---|---|---|---|---|---|
| | Thousands (1) | Per cent (2) | (3) | (4) | Thousands (5) | Per cent (6) | (7) | (8) |
| 1. British Columbia | 483 | 8.4 | −0.5 | +2.4 | 361 | 9.7 | +0.8 | +1.1 |
| 2. Ontario | 2,148 | 37.5 | +2.9 | +2.7 | 1,390 | 37.4 | +2.8 | +2.8 |
| 3. Alberta | 387 | 6.8 | −0.4 | +0.9 | 243 | 6.5 | −0.7 | +1.2 |
| 4. Saskatchewan | 324 | 5.7 | +0.1 | +0.1 | 202 | 5.5 | −0.1 | +0.3 |
| 5. Manitoba | 328 | 5.7 | +0.3 | −0.5 | 202 | 5.5 | +0.1 | −0.3 |
| 6. Quebec | 1,598 | 27.9 | −1.7 | −3.2 | 1,017 | 27.3 | −2.3 | −2.6 |
| 7. Nova Scotia | 243 | 4.2 | −0.2 | −1.2 | 162 | 4.4 | 0.0 | −1.4 |
| 8. New Brunswick | 180 | 3.1 | −0.4 | −0.9 | 119 | 3.2 | −0.3 | −1.0 |
| 9. P.E.I. | 37 | 0.7 | +0.1 | −0.4 | 23 | 0.6 | 0.0 | −0.3 |
| 10. Total | 5,728 | 100.0 | 6.6 | 12.3 | 3,719 | 100.0 | 7.1 | 11.0 |

SOURCE AND METHOD: Col 1: *Canada Year Book, 1959* (Ottawa, 1959), 730, 732, and *Census of Canada, 1951*, vol IV, Table 19. Provincial labour force estimates for 1956 were derived by inflating the 1951 census estimates of labour force, by industry, by the index of employment change, by industry, for 1956. The individual industry results were then totalled to give the provincial labour force estimates. These estimated provincial totals were compared with the total provincial labour force estimates for 1956 as recorded in the *Labour Force, Monthly, 1956* (DBS). These latter estimates are results of a monthly sample survey of the Canadian labour force. The major divergence occurred in the maritime provinces, where the former method appears to over-estimate the actual labour force for 1956 by approximately 8 per cent. The balance of the structural estimates diverged from the sample survey by less than 4 per cent with the overall difference being 2 per cent greater than the sample survey. Col 3: col 2 less col 4 of Table I-2; col 4: col 2 of Table I-3 less col 2 of Table I-5; col 5: *Census of Canada, 1951*, vol IV, Table 19; average earnings by age group, *Census of Canada, 1931*, vol V, 16; calculated by weighting the numbers in the labour force in each age bracket by the average earnings for this sex and age bracket relative to the average earnings of males in the 45-54 age bracket and totalling the results, for each province; Col 7: col 6 less col 4 of Table I-2; col 8: col 2 of difference, for, among persons with similar educational background, men earn on the average more than women,[8] adults earn more than children and young people, and among adult males earnings generally rise to a peak in the 45-54 year age group and then decline. To see how the quality of the labour force differs regionally, an "adult-male equivalent" measure was constructed for each province (Table I-5, col 5). The adult-male equivalent units were calculated by making an index of the average earnings over a year for each age group and sex, relative to the earnings of males in the age group 45-54 (the highest average earnings of any bracket for the majority of the provinces).[9] This index was then multiplied by the appropriate age groupings in the labour force, and the results were totalled. We would expect, other conditions being equal, that the association between the ratio of male-equivalents to total population and levels of service income per capita would be the same as that for the ratio of "unadjusted" labour force to total population, i.e., high ratios of the former should be associated with high levels of the latter. To show this association, the provincial shares of male-equivalent labour force were substracted from their respective shares in total population, and the resulting differences were totalled (disregarding signs). The deviations (col 7) confirmed our expectation of a positive association between this ratio and differing levels of service income per capita.

To measure the impact of correcting the labour force for varying demographic structures, the provincial shares of the male-equivalent labour force estimates were subtracted from the respective shares of service income. The total of the deviations (signs disregarded) appears in line 10, column 8. The first observation from these estimates is that a definite positive association between levels of adjusted service income per worker and rising levels of service income per capita exists, confirming our expectation of the relationship between these two variables. We can also conclude that, by adjusting the labour force for age-sex differences, the weighted inequality in service income per worker, 11.0, has been reduced by about a third over the original inequality in service income per capita, 16.3 (Table I-3, col 7, line 10). Thus, interprovincial differences in the quality of the labour force are important in explaining interprovincial inequalities in service income per capita.

The level of skill, measured by years of schooling completed per member of the labour force, was obtained (Table I-6) in order to investigate further the influence of quality differences in the labour force and their effect on differences in the level of service income. An examination of the differences in the levels of skill is important, because higher average earnings are directly related to higher levels of skill. Thus, if one province has a greater proportion of skilled than unskilled workers in its labour force, we would expect it to have a higher average service income per capita than a province in which the proportions are reversed. To obtain a clearer view of the relationship between years of schooling and levels of income per capita, the weighted average of years of schooling, by sex, for each province was calculated (cols 9 and 10); our main finding is that the quality,

TABLE I-6
Percentage of labour force with varying years of schooling and weighted average number of school years, by sex, for provinces, 1951

| Provinces in declining order of per capita income | Years of schooling | | | | | | | | Weighted average school years | |
|---|---|---|---|---|---|---|---|---|---|---|
| | 0-4 | | 5-8 | | 9-12 | | 13+ | | | |
| | M (1) | F (2) | M (3) | F (4) | M (5) | F (6) | M (7) | F (8) | M (9) | F (10) |
| 1. British Columbia | 5.7 | 1.6 | 35.5 | 18.9 | 47.6 | 63.1 | 11.2 | 16.4 | 9.10 | 10.35 |
| 2. Ontario | 5.5 | 2.1 | 44.4 | 27.9 | 38.0 | 52.9 | 12.2 | 17.2 | 8.82 | 9.99 |
| 3. Alberta | 8.1 | 3.0 | 41.7 | 21.1 | 42.0 | 59.9 | 8.2 | 16.1 | 8.51 | 10.14 |
| 4. Saskatchewan | 10.6 | 4.5 | 49.5 | 27.3 | 33.7 | 52.8 | 6.3 | 15.4 | 7.91 | 9.72 |
| 5. Manitoba | 10.0 | 5.0 | 43.4 | 27.0 | 39.2 | 57.9 | 7.4 | 10.1 | 8.25 | 9.45 |
| 6. Quebec | 9.3 | 3.7 | 54.4 | 42.2 | 28.0 | 46.1 | 8.4 | 8.0 | 7.93 | 8.86 |
| 7. Nova Scotia | 9.3 | 3.0 | 44.3 | 25.2 | 40.2 | 58.8 | 6.2 | 13.0 | 8.22 | 9.82 |
| 8. New Brunswick | 16.0 | 4.7 | 51.4 | 32.1 | 27.7 | 55.4 | 4.9 | 7.8 | 7.30 | 9.17 |
| 9. P.E.I. | 6.5 | 2.4 | 54.6 | 29.5 | 33.9 | 59.1 | 5.0 | 9.1 | 7.99 | 9.54 |

SOURCE AND METHOD: Cols 1-8: *Census of Canada, 1951*, vol IV, Table 19; cols 9 and 10: calculated by weighting the distribution of years of schooling by the following arbitrary year weights: class 0-4, weight 2.0; class 5-8, weight 6.5; class 9-12, weight 10.5; class 13+, weight 15.0. These weighted averages were then totalled.

in terms of years of schooling of the labour force, is positively associated with rising levels of per capita income. However, since the weight assigned to years of schooling was arbitrary, and since their exact effect on service income is not known, no direct measurement of the impact of inequality arising out of this factor is possible.

Thus, even when service rather than total income differentials were considered and even when a shift from per capita of total population to per worker was made, there was still an inequality of 11.0 (line 10, col 8 of Table I-5). Part of the explanation for this inequality may lie in the age-sex-education differentials which cannot be adequately quantified and also to intersectoral differences that may partly reflect the age-sex-education differentials, and partly to other variables. We will go on, then, to study the impact of these sectoral differentials on interprovincial income inequality.

Unfortunately the Canadian national accounts data do not show such a breakdown by provinces. It was necessary to shift the analysis of interprovincial differences in per capita income from a discussion of the influence of various types of income on inequality to a discussion of share differences in gross value added per worker (for a full explanation of the method of estimating gross value added by sector by province see appendix B). Since the gross value added estimates include such items as undistributed corporation profits and capital consumption allowances and exclude transfer payments and interest on the public debt, they are not directly comparable to personal income estimates. Thus, only by inference can we learn something about per capita income differentials from differentials in gross value added per worker. However, gross value added per worker is an important source of information, and so its use seems justified in the analysis of interprovincial differences in per capita income.

## SHARE DIFFERENTIALS IN GROSS VALUE ADDED AMONG PROVINCES

The nine sectors set out for examination of the distribution of production between provinces are shown in Table I-7. The first conclusion that can be drawn from this table, most evident if we look at the three subtotals of GVA (i.e., A, M, and S sectors, lines 1, 5, and 9), is that the shares vary more widely for the A and M sectors than for the S sector. The main reason for the wider variation in the first two is the wide dispersion of shares in agriculture, forestry, mining, and manufacturing output. In contrast, the majority of output shares grouped under the S sector showed a relatively greater uniformity among the nine provinces. The explanation is simple. In the case of the A sector (agriculture, forestry, and fishing) and of mining in the M sector (these industries are resource based), production is localized according to the spatial distribution of resources: the prairies, with abundant flat land and sparse population, produce wheat; the maritime provinces (on both coasts) specialize in fishing; a mineral-rich province

## TABLE I-7
Percentage distribution of GVA for the three main sectors, and their components by provinces, 1956

| Sectors | Provinces in declining order of per capita income | | | | | | | | | | |
| --- | --- | --- | --- | --- | --- | --- | --- | --- | --- | --- | --- |
| | British Columbia (1) | Ontario (2) | Alberta (3) | Saskatchewan (4) | Manitoba (5) | Quebec (6) | Nova Scotia (7) | New Brunswick (8) | P.E.I. (9) | Unweighted mean 1 to 9 (10) | Weighted mean 1 to 9 (11) |
| 1. *A sector* | 12.9 | 5.4 | 17.5 | 38.5 | 14.5 | 6.4 | 7.1 | 13.0 | 21.3 | 15.2 | 10.1 |
| 2.  Agriculture | 2.5 | 4.2 | 16.8 | 38.0 | 13.5 | 3.5 | 2.9 | 5.4 | 17.6 | 11.6 | 7.2 |
| 3.  Forestry | 9.3 | 1.1 | 0.6 | 0.3 | 0.7 | 2.9 | 1.6 | 6.5 | — | 2.6 | 2.5 |
| 4.  Fishing and trapping | 1.2 | 0.1 | 0.1 | 0.2 | 0.4 | 0.1 | 2.6 | 1.1 | 3.7 | 1.1 | 0.4 |
| 5. *M sector* | 44.6 | 53.1 | 44.7 | 23.6 | 31.7 | 50.1 | 30.4 | 30.6 | 14.8 | 36.0 | 46.7 |
| 6.  Mining | 3.5 | 2.1 | 15.9 | 4.6 | 1.9 | 3.1 | 5.1 | 1.7 | — | 4.3 | 3.8 |
| 7.  Construction | 15.1 | 9.5 | 16.9 | 12.1 | 11.1 | 9.8 | 8.8 | 11.2 | 9.3 | 11.5 | 11.0 |
| 8.  Manufacturing | 26.1 | 41.5 | 11.9 | 6.9 | 18.8 | 37.2 | 16.4 | 17.7 | 5.6 | 20.2 | 31.9 |
| 9. *S sector* | 42.5 | 41.5 | 37.8 | 37.9 | 53.8 | 43.5 | 62.5 | 56.4 | 63.9 | 48.8 | 43.3 |
| 10.  Utilities | 1.9 | 2.0 | 1.4 | 1.3 | 1.9 | 2.2 | 1.9 | 1.8 | 0.9 | 1.7 | 1.9 |
| 11.  Transport and communications | 7.8 | 6.6 | 6.8 | 8.9 | 12.5 | 8.4 | 11.3 | 14.4 | 11.1 | 9.8 | 8.0 |
| 12.  Commerce | 12.3 | 11.6 | 11.8 | 11.3 | 12.9 | 11.9 | 14.9 | 15.3 | 18.5 | 13.4 | 12.0 |
| 13.  Finance | 6.0 | 6.8 | 4.3 | 3.7 | 8.0 | 6.5 | 4.7 | 5.0 | 4.6 | 5.5 | 6.2 |
| 14.  Service | 8.3 | 8.2 | 7.6 | 8.2 | 10.6 | 9.5 | 14.9 | 12.0 | 14.8 | 10.4 | 8.9 |
| 15.  Government | 6.2 | 6.3 | 5.9 | 4.5 | 7.9 | 5.0 | 14.9 | 7.8 | 13.9 | 8.0 | 6.3 |

SOURCE AND METHOD: A and M sectors: Dominion Bureau of Statistics, *Survey of Production, 1961* (Ottawa, 1961), 16; S sector: Dominion Bureau of Statistics, *Canada Year Book, 1961* (Ottawa, 1961) – data were collected from various tables throughout the publication relating to the subsectors of like Alberta devotes large amounts of resources to mining. Manufacturing also tends to be localized, especially near its largest markets, to reduce transportation costs and to obtain the benefits of large-scale production (e.g., note the large shares of manufacturing output in British Columbia, Ontario, and Quebec, all provinces with large populations). The surpluses from these areas are then exported to the other regions. In contrast, the products of the various divisions of the S sector, as well as construction in the M sector, tend to be consumed locally. In many cases these products cannot bear transport costs and are generally produced in limited amounts in all regions. For example, transportation facilities are required by all regions regardless of the type of production carried on in the other two sectors, commerce (i.e., retail and wholesale trade) serves the local market, and construction, a large part of which is residential construction, is used locally.

The questions which now arise are how are the output shares of the A and M sectors (i.e., those main sectors with a clearly defined range of output shares) associated with varying levels of income per capita, and what are the implications if such an association exists. Lines 1 and 5 of Table I-7 show that, for the A sector, the association, if we consider the top two (British Columbia and Ontario) and the bottom two (New Brunswick and Prince Edward Island) per capita income provinces, is negative, while for the M sector it is positive. This type of conclusion is what we have come to expect from observations of international differences in output shares as they are related to per capita income differences: those countries with the highest per capita incomes are generally those with the smallest amount of resources devoted to agricultural production. However, a significant difference between the international comparisons and these interprovincial differences is evident: the prairie provinces all show per capita incomes equal to or greater than the median level. The conclusion, then, is that the level of output per man must be higher for this type of agricultural production than for that observed either in low income countries or in low income provinces in Canada.[10] Further, high income provinces tend to have either a large manufacturing sector (where output per worker is high) or a large share of output concentrated in a relatively high productivity resource output (e.g., agriculture, forestry, or mining). In contrast, provinces at the bottom of the income scale are deficient in both. Thus, not only is the distribution of resources between agricultural and non-agricultural output important, but the composition and productivity within these sectors appear to be crucial determinants of income differences.

The role of the S sector in explaining these differences in provincial per capita incomes is not as obvious because of the lack of clear association between levels of income and differences in the shares of output of the various subsectors of the S sector. The only point that does emerge from Table I-7 (lines 11, 14, and 15) is that the lower income provinces tend to show slightly larger shares of output for transportation, personal service, and government operation. This could simply be a result of the lack of large output levels in the A and M sectors for these regions.[11]

Lastly, comparing the unweighted means of the sectoral shares with the weighted means brings out an interesting contrast. For the A sector the weighted mean is lower than the unweighted mean, while the opposite is true for the M sector. This indicates that provinces which account for large shares in total output have below average shares in A sector production but above average shares in M sector output, a reflection of the earlier finding of the associations between the shares of these sectors in total output and levels of per capita income.

INDUSTRIAL DISTRIBUTION OF THE LABOUR FORCE AND
RELATIVE OUTPUT PER WORKER BY PROVINCE

To amplify the findings on the distribution of output among provinces and its relation to income differences, the allocation of labour force among the same eleven sectors was derived (Table I-8). The basic data for Table I-8 were collected from the 1951 census. These data were then extrapolated forward to 1956 by a series of industrial employment indices which appear annually in the *Canada Year Book*. These figures were then adjusted for the regional increase in total labour force to obtain the closest possible approximation to each region's labour force.

The first conclusion that can be reached from this distribution of the labour force is that the main results observed for the distribution of GVA in Table I-7 are repeated in Table I-8: the range of shares in the A and M sectors is wider than for the S sector, and the associations between these shares and levels of income are the same. However, one important difference between the two distributions does appear, and that is the much wider range in shares of labour force within sectors than for similar output shares. For example, the labour force shares for agriculture (line 2), for British Columbia and Prince Edward Island range from approximately 11 percent for the former to 41 per cent, or about 3.7 to 1 for the latter, while the output shares (Table I-7, line 2, cols 1 and 9) vary only from 13 to 21 per cent, approximately 1.6 to 1. Similar differences can be found for other sectors. Also in Table I-8 we note that the relationship between the unweighted and weighted means is the same as in the case of output shares: the provinces with large shares of total labour force tend to have below average shares of labour force in the A sector and above average shares in the M sector.

Table I-9 was constructed to clarify further this relation between differences in the shares of GVA and labour force within provinces. The figures for lines 1-14 were derived by dividing the output share for a particular sector by the corresponding sectoral share of labour force. This yields a *ratio* of product per worker

# TABLE I-8

Percentage distribution of the labour force for the three main sectors and their components, by provinces, 1956

| Sectors | British Columbia (1) | Ontario (2) | Alberta (3) | Saskatchewan (4) | Manitoba (5) | Quebec (6) | Nova Scotia (7) | New Brunswick (8) | P.E.I. (9) | Unweighted mean 1 to 9 (10) | Weighted mean 1 to 9 (11) |
|---|---|---|---|---|---|---|---|---|---|---|---|
| | | | | Provinces in declining order of per capita income | | | | | | | |
| 1. *A sector* | 10.9 | 10.6 | 30.2 | 46.0 | 23.2 | 14.8 | 15.6 | 24.6 | 40.5 | 24.0 | 16.9 |
| 2. Agriculture | 5.7 | 9.6 | 29.5 | 45.4 | 22.3 | 12.1 | 9.6 | 14.8 | 35.4 | 20.5 | 14.2 |
| 3. Forestry | 4.2 | 0.9 | 0.4 | 0.2 | 0.4 | 2.3 | 2.0 | 7.3 | 0.6 | 2.0 | 1.7 |
| 4. Fishing and trapping | 1.0 | 0.1 | 0.3 | 0.4 | 0.5 | 0.3 | 4.0 | 2.5 | 4.5 | 1.5 | 1.0 |
| 5. *M sector* | 31.7 | 40.4 | 22.2 | 11.0 | 23.4 | 39.3 | 31.4 | 25.8 | 16.4 | 26.8 | 34.8 |
| 6. Mining | 2.6 | 1.6 | 4.5 | 0.6 | 1.3 | 1.4 | 7.1 | 0.7 | 0.1 | 2.2 | 2.5 |
| 7. Construction | 6.3 | 7.3 | 7.9 | 4.2 | 6.2 | 7.6 | 8.0 | 6.6 | 6.0 | 6.7 | 7.0 |
| 8. Manufacturing | 22.7 | 31.5 | 9.8 | 6.2 | 15.9 | 30.3 | 16.3 | 18.5 | 10.3 | 17.9 | 25.2 |
| 9. *S sector* | 57.4 | 49.0 | 47.7 | 43.0 | 53.3 | 46.0 | 53.1 | 49.6 | 43.1 | 49.1 | 48.2 |
| 10. Utilities | 1.2 | 1.8 | 1.1 | 0.7 | 1.3 | 1.0 | 1.3 | 1.1 | 0.7 | 1.1 | 1.3 |
| 11. Transport and communications | 9.4 | 6.8 | 7.7 | 8.2 | 10.0 | 7.4 | 8.3 | 10.3 | 6.2 | 8.3 | 7.6 |
| 12. Commerce | 17.1 | 15.0 | 14.1 | 12.3 | 16.9 | 12.7 | 14.5 | 14.4 | 12.6 | 14.4 | 14.2 |
| 13. Finance | 3.6 | 3.5 | 2.4 | 1.7 | 3.2 | 2.9 | 1.7 | 1.8 | 1.3 | 2.5 | 2.9 |
| 14. Service and government | 26.2 | 21.9 | 22.4 | 20.1 | 22.0 | 22.0 | 27.3 | 22.0 | 22.3 | 22.9 | 22.2 |

NOTE: See note to Table I-5 regarding the relationship between these labour force estimates and the ones obtained by the Dominion Bureau of Statistics in their monthly sample survey of the labour force.

SOURCE AND METHOD: Cols 1 to 9: *Census of Canada, 1951*, vol IV, Table 16, and indices to bring data up to 1956 are from *Canada Year Book, 1959*, 700, 732; col 11: calculated by adding the share, weighted by the distribution of total labour force between the provinces.

TABLE I-9

Relative output per worker and a measure of intersectoral inequality by provinces, 1956

| Sectors | Provinces in declining order of per capita income | | | | | | | | | Unweighted mean 1 to 9 (10) | Weighted mean 1 to 9 (11) |
| | British Columbia (1) | Ontario (2) | Alberta (3) | Saskatchewan (4) | Manitoba (5) | Quebec (6) | Nova Scotia (7) | New Brunswick (8) | P.E.I. (9) | | |
|---|---|---|---|---|---|---|---|---|---|---|---|
| 1. *A sector* | 1.18 | 0.51 | 0.58 | 0.84 | 0.63 | 0.43 | 0.46 | 0.53 | 0.53 | 0.63 | 0.59 |
| 2. Agriculture | 0.44 | 0.44 | 0.57 | 0.84 | 0.60 | 0.28 | 0.30 | 0.36 | 0.50 | 0.48 | 0.51 |
| 3. Forestry | 2.20 | 1.19 | 1.75 | 1.67 | 1.86 | 1.25 | 0.82 | 0.89 | — | 1.29 | 1.45 |
| 4. Fishing and trapping | 1.17 | 0.82 | 0.32 | 0.56 | 0.71 | 0.25 | 0.64 | 0.46 | 0.82 | 0.64 | 0.37 |
| 5. *M sector* | 1.41 | 1.31 | 2.01 | 2.15 | 1.35 | 1.27 | 0.97 | 1.19 | 0.90 | 1.40 | 1.34 |
| 6. Mining | 1.33 | 1.30 | 3.54 | 7.68 | 1.41 | 2.28 | 0.72 | 2.33 | — | 2.29 | 1.51 |
| 7. Construction | 2.39 | 1.31 | 2.15 | 2.85 | 1.80 | 1.28 | 1.10 | 1.69 | 1.52 | 1.79 | 1.58 |
| 8. Manufacturing | 1.15 | 1.32 | 1.21 | 1.12 | 1.18 | 1.23 | 1.01 | 0.96 | 0.54 | 1.08 | 1.26 |
| 9. *S sector* | 0.74 | 0.85 | 1.79 | 0.88 | 1.01 | 0.95 | 1.18 | 1.14 | 1.48 | 1.00 | 0.90 |
| 10. Transport and communications | 0.84 | 0.97 | 0.88 | 1.08 | 1.25 | 1.13 | 1.36 | 1.40 | 1.78 | 1.19 | 1.48 |
| 11. Utilities | 1.58 | 1.10 | 1.31 | 1.94 | 1.46 | 2.29 | 1.43 | 1.66 | 1.29 | 1.56 | 1.05 |
| 12. Commerce | 0.72 | 0.78 | 0.84 | 0.92 | 0.76 | 0.94 | 1.03 | 1.06 | 1.47 | 0.95 | 0.85 |
| 13. Finance | 1.68 | 1.95 | 1.79 | 2.15 | 2.51 | 2.26 | 2.71 | 2.82 | 3.48 | 2.37 | 2.09 |
| 14. Service and government | 0.55 | 0.66 | 0.60 | 0.63 | 0.84 | 0.66 | 1.09 | 0.90 | 1.29 | 0.80 | 0.69 |
| 15. $A/(M + S)$ | 1.21 | 0.48 | 0.49 | 0.74 | 0.57 | 0.39 | 0.42 | 0.46 | 0.40 | | |
| 16. Measure of inequality | 42.8 | 32.8 | 49.9 | 32.0 | 33.0 | 34.3 | 20.9 | 29.1 | 48.0 | | |

METHOD: Calculated by dividing the output share data of Table I-7 by the labour force share data of Table I-8. The measure of inequality shown in in the sector to product per worker for each province as a whole. The average product per worker for all sectors in each province is 1. Thus, we are able to judge whether a particular sector exceeds or falls short of the provincial average. From the table we can conclude that the A sector is generally below provincial averages (British Columbia is an exception), while the M and S sectors are near or above the average. The differences are shown clearly by the weighted and unweighted means for each sector (cols 10 and 11). These results conform to observations of intersectoral differences in product per worker among countries.[12]

Another interesting result of these intersectoral differences is the relative widening in the relation between the A and non-A sectors as we move towards lower income per capita provinces, another indication of the differences in levels of relative output per worker in the A sector (particularly in agriculture) that exist among provinces. These declining relatives reveal that the interprovincial differences in agricultural output per man are greater than differences in output per man in the non-agriculture sectors. If output per worker were the same in all sectors, unlike these results, then in each province the sectoral shares in labour force and the sectoral shares in GVA would be the same. If the share distributions were unequal, the differences would represent the weighted measure of inequality (weighted by the share of each sector in the labour force). If the differences were totalled (disregarding signs), the results would yield a measure of inequality for each province. Such calculations were made and are shown in line 16 of Table I-9. The calculations are composed of the addition of differences for all sectors for which data are available (sectors shown in Tables I-7 and I-8).

Our expectations are that the level of intersectoral inequality will vary inversely with levels of income per capita. The results, as shown in line 16 of Table I-9, neither confirm nor reject this hypothesis. However, the lowest income province does show the second highest level of inequality. The explanation for the large measures of inequality for British Columbia and Alberta may be that both provinces are active in resource exploitation, where the output per worker levels are high compared to the remaining sectors in those provinces. On the whole, however, the expectation of higher levels of inequality for low income provinces is not met. This may be the result of large and inconsistent differences in the shares of the A sector between high and low income provinces.

## CONSEQUENCES OF INTER- AND INTRASECTORAL PRODUCT PER WORKER DIFFERENTIALS ON THE LEVEL OF PERSONAL INCOME PER WORKER

In the discussion so far on the causes of income differentials among provinces, two elements have played an important role in this explanation: intersectoral and intrasectoral inequality differences in per worker product. To ascertain the approximate importance of each element in explaining these differences, Table I-10 was constructed. The information on the contribution of intrasectoral product per worker was obtained by standardizing, at the national level, the weighted labour force distribution between the eleven sectors under review. These averages were then multiplied by the adjusted relative output per worker for each of the sectors (i.e., each per worker relative was multiplied by the corresponding provincial level of relative personal income per worker,[13] col 1). The two figures were then multiplied and the results totalled (col 2). The resultant relatives give us a measure of the intrasectoral effect, in differences in income levels: they show us how each province stands, relative to the national average, in the contribution of intrasectoral product per worker to its observed relative personal income per worker level. To obtain a similar set of relatives for the contribution of intersectoral product per worker to differences in per worker personal income, the weighted national average of relative output per worker for the eleven sectors was multiplied by provincial distributions of the labour force. These results were then totalled and appear in column 3. To make these two relatives comparable to the weighted inequalities in total personal income per worker (col 7),[14] the relatives of columns 2 and 3 were mutiplied by the respective provincial shares in total labour force, and the results were adjusted to total 100 per cent. The labour force shares (col 2, Table I-5) were then subtracted from these weighted shares of intrasectoral and intersectoral product per worker and the deviations totalled (disregarding signs).

An important result which emerges from these calculations is the mixed pattern of deviation signs between intrasectoral and intersectoral product per worker. In fact, of the nine provinces under study, three (Alberta, Saskatchewan, and Quebec) show a difference in sign. Of these provinces, two (Saskatchewan and Quebec) are especially interesting cases. In the former we noted earlier that in spite of its great reliance on agricultural output it was counted among the high income provinces. At the time, it was suggested that this probably occurred because it enjoyed a relatively high output per worker in this sector. This now seems confirmed. Conversely, in the case of Quebec where the distribution of output is much less concentrated, it was observed that its agricultural sector lagged far behind comparably structured provinces (Ontario and British Columbia) in output per worker in this sector. This intrasectoral differential appears now to be one of the factors causing Quebec to fall behind the other two in total income per capita.

Our main interest, however, is in separating the contribution of intra- and intersectoral output per worker to the total inequality in income per worker. As a first step towards making this calculation, columns 4 and 5 were added for each province (col 6) as well as the total for each column (line 10). The province by province totals were calculated to indicate that intra- and intersectoral output per worker do add, approximately, to the actual difference for each province. The total for weighted intersectoral differences (5.4) was then divided by the

# TABLE I-10

A comparison of the contribution of intra- and intersectoral product per worker to differences in provincial income per worker, 1956

| Provinces in declining order of personal income per worker | Relative personal income per worker (1) | Intra-sectoral product per worker (2) | Inter-sectoral product per worker (3) | Weighted differences | | | Weighted inequality in total income per worker (7) |
|---|---|---|---|---|---|---|---|
| | | | | Col 2 minus col 2 of Table I-5 (4) | Col 3 minus col 2 of Table I-5 (5) | Col 4 + col 5 (6) | |
| 1. British Columbia | 137.43 | 132.14 | 107.16 | +1.2 | +0.4 | +1.6 | +2.4 |
| 2. Alberta | 122.07 | 128.09 | 92.40 | +1.5 | −0.7 | +0.8 | +0.8 |
| 3. Ontario | 113.13 | 107.63 | 107.02 | +0.9 | +1.5 | +2.4 | +2.6 |
| 4. Saskatchewan | 108.94 | 138.47 | 79.71 | +1.8 | −1.3 | +0.5 | +0.0 |
| 5. Manitoba | 98.60 | 104.47 | 96.34 | 0.0 | −0.4 | −0.4 | −0.5 |
| 6. Quebec | 92.46 | 91.00 | 105.96 | −3.7 | +0.8 | −2.9 | −3.2 |
| 7. Nova Scotia | 82.40 | 82.73 | 100.22 | −0.9 | −0.1 | −1.0 | −1.1 |
| 8. New Brunswick | 82.12 | 86.54 | 99.65 | −0.5 | −0.1 | −0.6 | −0.8 |
| 9. P.E.I. | 62.29 | 64.54 | 81.94 | −0.3 | −0.1 | −0.4 | −0.3 |
| 10. Total (disregarding signs) | | | | 10.8 | 5.4 | 10.6 | 11.7 |

SOURCE AND METHOD: Data from Tables I-8 and I-9. Col 1: col 1 of Table I-2, divided by col 1 of Table I-5. The resulting ratios were then divided by their unweighted countrywide mean. Col 2: constructed by multiplying the weighted national average of labour force shares (Table I-8) for each sector by the relative income per worker for each sector, by provinces. These relatives were first weighted by the provincial income per worker relative. The results were then totalled. Col 3: constructed by multiplying the weighted national averages of relative output per worker (Table I-9) by sectors by the provincial shares of labour force. The results were then totalled. Col 4: col 2, weighted by provincial labour force distribution (col 2, Table I-5) and adjusted to equal 100 per cent, less col 2, Table I-5. Col 5: col 3 weighted by provincial labour force distribution (col 2, Table I-5) and adjusted to equal 100 per cent, less col 2, Table I-5. Col 6: col 4 plus col 5; col 7: col 2, of Table I-2 less col 2 of Table I-5; line 10: total, disregarding signs.

total for columns 4 and 5 (16.2). The resulting calculation shows that inter-sectoral differences account for a third of the total interprovincial difference in income.[15] Clearly, then, intersectoral differences in shares of the different sectors in the labour force play an important role in explaining differing levels of per capita income among provinces.

# 2
# Long-term Changes in National and Regional Gross Value Added, Population, and Labour Force, Selected Years 1890-1956

THE FOCUS in this chapter shifts from a cross-section view of regional income inequality to an examination of the relationship between long-term changes in national growth and its spatial distribution. The main benefits of this different approach are that we can study the relationship between periods of national development and levels and rates of regional growth and, simultaneously, observe how the parameters connecting these two units change when we shift from a simple spatial interaction to a time-space connection.

Most long-term development studies have concentrated either on national variables or on the growth of individual regions (the latter type often includes comparative descriptions of regional performance). Here an attempt is made to specifically integrate national growth with regional deviations. It is obvious that the growth of geographically large countries represents a blend of many different regional fortunes. Thus, in Canada, we should expect a wide variety of regional levels and rates of economic performance because of the differences between regions in resource endowments, locational advantages, cultural influences, periods of settlement, etc. A refocusing on regions and national economic growth is thus essential in the Canadian case.

The period covered in this study is from 1890 to 1956, and even for this short period only four years are investigated. The choice of the four years was somewhat arbitrary. First, income measures of any type (see chapter one) are not available before 1926. Second, the only comprehensive and relatively consistent records of regional (provincial) economic performance before 1926 are the decennial censuses. Third, since the primary interest in this study was in trend relations—average changes over periods longer than business cycles—in national and regional growth, the points had to bear some relationship to broadly defined "phases" of Canadian development. Fourthly, if the cyclical influence were to be eliminated, then the years chosen for study had to relate as closely as possible to similar phases of the business cycle. If this last prescription is not fulfilled one runs the risk of biasing, up or down, the trend rates of growth: if the initial year fell in the trough of a business cycle and the terminal at the peak, then an upward bias in the rate might occur. These four considerations led to the selection of 1890, 1910, 1929, and 1956 as the four points of national and regional observation.

Although, in historical terms, the period chosen here is relatively short (66 years), it nevertheless embraces at least two important segments of Canadian economic development. The first we might call the "frontier phase" which stretches from 1890 to 1910. The second, the "maturity phase," 1910 to 1956.[1] The separation point is somewhat artificial, but it does serve to separate quite different regional development patterns and, from this point of view, is useful.

NATIONAL GROWTH TRENDS, 1890-1956

*Total Gross Value Added*

Simon Kuznets has stated that "the distinctive characteristic of modern economic growth is the combination of high rates of increase in population with high rates of increase in per capita product—with the obvious implication of enormous increases in total product."[2] A logical point to start our discussion of national change over this 66-year period, then, is with changes in total output. A view of this is provided in Table II-1.

TABLE II-1

Percentage rates of change, gross value added in 1935-9 prices, Canada, and gross national product in 1954 prices, United States, for selected periods, 1890-1956

| | Gross value added, Canada | | Gross national product, U.S. |
| --- | --- | --- | --- |
| Interval | Change for whole period (1) | Annual average (2) | Annual average (3) |
| 1890-1910 | 117.2 | 4.0 | — |
| 1910-29 | 86.3 | 3.3 | 2.8 |
| 1929-56 | 188.3 | 4.0 | 3.0 |
| 1890-1956 | 1066.9 | 3.8 | — |
| 1910-56 | 437.2 | 3.7 | 2.9 |

SOURCE AND METHOD:   Calculations for cols 1 and 2 are based on Table II-4, line 1. Annual averages, here and in all subsequent tables unless otherwise noted, are in compound rates of growth. U.S. data from E. F. Denison, *The Sources of Economic Growth in the United States*, Supplementary Paper 13, Committee for Economic Development (1962), 17.

According to the estimates presented in the table Canadian total gross value added increased over 1,000-fold (in constant dollar terms, col 1) between 1890 and 1956, a quite impressive change in the size of the Canadian economy. This expansion, however, did not proceed steadily. Dividing the 66 years into frontier and maturity phases, it is evident that the former embraces a period of substantial growth in the productive capacity of the economy. The latter is more mixed and is comprised of a slower growth period, 1910 to 1929, and a rapid period, 1929 to 1956. These variations are brought out even more clearly by an examination of the annual compound growth rates (col 2). Note also that there is apparently no long-term diminution in the expansion of total output. The regional reallocation of economic activity which accompanied these national aggregates is important and will be discussed later. To add more perspective to the magnitude of the changes in the national economy, comparable growth rates to total GNP for the United States have been shown in column 3. For all periods compared, the Canadian growth rates exceeded those of the United States. Canadian expansion in total output has been impressive, and we can assume that regional changes have played an important role in this expansion.

## Population and Per Capita Gross Value Added

The principle barometer of modern economic growth, assumed in Kuznets' statement, is the conjuncture of rapidly growing per capita product and population, regardless of the type of country undergoing modern economic growth. The question thus raised is: Do rapid increases in average product and population accompany modern growth in countries of recent settlement–such as Canada– where initial population expansion comes from international migration, as well as in older "traditional" economies, where population growth is primarily through variations in natural increase?

Table II-2 has been constructed to assist in answering this question in the affirmative. Newly settled countries follow the general description of economic growth in modern periods, having a high growth in average product and population. Over the 66-year period the annual growth in each was close to 2.0 per cent. Rapid expansion in total and per capita product and in total population have been part of the Canadian process of development since 1890.

Several other features of Canadian development are evident from the data in Table II-2. (a) The long-term movements in population are not similar to those of gross value added (Table II-1), in constant prices, in two respects. First, population, unlike gross value added, shows a distinct retardation in its growth rate. Thus, by the last period (1929-56), the rate of population growth was approximately a fifth below that of the first period. Second, population growth does not show any tendency towards long-term fluctuations as does the movement of GVA, which showed distinct variations in its rate of growth for these three periods. Possibly, however, a finer breakdown in population totals, say rates of change of annual figures, might bring out long swings such as we noted for total output.[3] (*b*) In comparing the growth in total population with total output (Table II-1), note that in the first two periods the two rates show complementary movements: both show rapid growth in the first period and a distinctly slower rate of growth in the second period. The last period, however, exhibits the opposite relationship: a high rate of growth in total GVA, while population growth is the lowest for the 66-year period. (*c*) Annual rates of growth in GVA (1935-9 prices) per capita show two interesting movements. First, there is a definite long-term rise in the rate of growth in per capita output; in fact, the annual rate of growth in the last period is a quarter higher than it was in the first period. Second, the movement has not been steadily upward, but has been marked by variations in the rate of growth of per capita product (Table II-2 shows the first and last period exhibit relatively high rates of growth compared to the middle period).

What do these trends imply about Canadian development? First, the steady rise in per capita product is clear evidence that living standards in Canada have increased over this 66-year period. As a result, the people in Canada have been continually freed from purchasing only necessities–food, clothing, houses–and their spectrum of alternative choices has widened. This means simply that demand for goods with a high income elasticity of demand gradually took precedence over those with a low elasticity. What impact this has had on the location and structure of production will be studied later. Second, the discovery of the rapid expansion in average product, especially during the frontier settle-

TABLE II-2

Percentage rates of change in population and gross value added in 1935-9 prices, per capita, Canada, selected periods, 1890-1956

| Interval | Population | GVA per capita | Level of GVA (1935-9 prices) per capita | |
|---|---|---|---|---|
| | annual average (1) | annual average (2) | Year | GVA per capita (3) |
| 1890-1910 | 2.1 | 1.9 | 1890 | $268 |
| 1910-29 | 1.8 | 1.5 | 1910 | $388 |
| 1929-56 | 1.7 | 2.3 | 1929 | $516 |
| 1890-1956 | 1.8 | 1.9 | 1956 | $953 |
| 1910-56 | 1.7 | 2.0 | | |

SOURCE AND METHOD:　Col 1: for the years 1890 and 1910 from the *Census of Canada, 1931*, vol I, 388-92. For 1929 and 1956 from annual estimates of population based on births, deaths, immigration and emigration published annually in the *Canada Year Book*. Col 3: appendix B divided, respectively, by the following population estimates (000 omitted): 1891, 4,769; 1911, 7,156; 1929, 10,016; 1956, 15,635.

ment period, is interesting, for it opens the whole field of inquiry into the connection between expanding new regions and the older settled regions. Again, more of this will appear later.

## Labour Force and GVA Per Worker

The previous section has outlined the trends in output per unit of total population. However, we are also interested in changes in productivity, measured very crudely as output per unit of unadjusted labour input (unadjusted for quality or hours of work). Two connections are involved in this simple shift from per capita to per worker output: the first involves the relationship between the size of the labour force component in total population, and the second the trend changes in output per worker.

Table II-3 presents a view of both these trends. Beginning with the share of labour force in total population (col 2), we should inquire what relationship exists between total labour force and total population. One tie-in is obvious: the size of the labour force component is related to the age-sex structure of the population, and the more people in the population who are of working age the greater the potential size of the labour force. In a closed stable population we could expect very few changes in the population age structure and little variation in potential labour force. Canada is not a closed population system but an open one, therefore the potential labour force–given the age-sex selectivity of migration–can be expected to show variations through time.

Actual labour force, defined by the census as all persons (10 and over up to 1931 and 14 and over since) normally engaged in an occupation, whether employed or not employed, may differ from potential labour force because of the total demand for labour and the structure of this demand (for skilled versus unskilled labour, for men versus women, etc.). The interaction of these supply and demand factors will determine the level of labour force per capita.

Column 2 of Table II-3 gives some indication of the trend in these labour force ratios. A rise, although not steady, is evident over the 66-year period, and two factors seem to be important. First, for the early decades, especially in the period of frontier settlement, large-scale immigration forced the ratio up by increasing the share of population in the working-age range. In this case the heavy inflow of foreign-born added proportionately more to labour force than to population. Second, a change in the composition of the labour force is evident. As the economy matured (here, after 1910) the structure of labour demand shifted. Economic maturity meant a better trained labour force was required, and the result was that young people entered the labour force later in life. This change can be seen in the decreasing participation ratios for both males and females in the 10-14 age bracket. Next, as the economy became more industrialized and factory pension plans more numerous, retirement from the labour force after age 60 became more prevalent (see trends in participation ratios for

TABLE II-3

Labour force, participation rates and GVA (1935-9 prices) per worker, Canada, selected years 1890-1956

| Year | Labour force (thousands) (1) | Per cent of (1) to total population (2) | GVA per worker (3) | Interval | Per cent rate of increase per year | |
|---|---|---|---|---|---|---|
| | | | | | Labour force (4) | GVA per worker (5) |
| 1890 | 1,595 | 33.7 | 801 | 1890-1910 | 2.7 | 1.2 |
| 1910 | 2,724 | 38.1 | 1,018 | 1910-1929 | 2.1 | 1.2 |
| 1929 | 4,116 | 41.1 | 1,256 | 1929-1956 | 1.3 | 2.7 |
| 1956 | 5,729 | 37.0 | 2,601 | | | |
| | | | | 1890-1956 | 2.0 | 1.8 |
| | | | | 1910-1956 | 1.6 | 2.1 |

SOURCE AND METHOD: Col 1: appendix C; col 2: col 1 divided by population estimates in note to Table II-2; col 3: Tables II-4 and II-7.

Participation rates by age and sex, Canada, 1911, 1931, and 1951

| Age | Male | | | Age | Female | | |
|---|---|---|---|---|---|---|---|
| | 1911 | 1931 | 1951 | | 1911 | 1931 | 1951 |
| 10-14 | 4.8 | 3.1 | 1.3 | 10-14 | 2.3 | 0.5 | 0.4 |
| 15-24 | 84.4 | 75.0 | 74.9 | 15-24 | 27.8 | 33.3 | 42.3 |
| 25-64 | 96.2 | 96.5 | 94.4 | 25-64 | 12.1 | 15.3 | 21.4 |
| 65+ | 69.4 | 55.7 | 38.7 | 65+ | 5.5 | 6.2 | 5.1 |

SOURCE AND METHOD:    Appendix A, Table A-3.

men and women over 65, especially after 1931). Lastly, a more industrialized, higher income economy provides a wider variety of job opportunities for women plus release from many household duties. These combined supply-demand influences served to increase dramatically female participation rates. The joint result has been to expand the share of labour force in total population.

But how have these "supply" factors affected the growth of the labour force, and how have they influenced growth of output per worker? The first question is quite easy to answer. The annual percentage change in the labour force (col 4) follows a long-term trend similar to the growth in population, showing a steady retardation in the rate of growth through time. Also, the rate of growth of the labour force has been greater than that of population. The relationship between the growth and composition (here the age-sex specific participation ratios) of the labour force and the change in output per worker is more complicated. Before a detailed discussion on this relationship begins it might be well to set out the three assumptions which underlie the "productivity" measure shown in column 5.

The first is that the level of unemployment in each year is constant; second, the number of man-hours expended annually has been constant; third, the quality of the labour force has remained unchanged.

It is impossible to deal here in detail with the first assumption, except to point out that the preliminary findings by Professor Kuznets for long-term changes in per worker GNP indicate that "the allowance for unemployment does not affect significantly the longer term trends in product per worker or per man-hour."[4] The same, however, cannot be said for the failure to adjust output per man-year to output per man-hour, for the decline in hours worked per week has been quite substantial. In fact, Firestone estimates that between 1870 and 1950 the decline in hours worked per week in manufacturing by wage earners was something like twenty-two.[5] The result of standardizing for man-hours worked was to increase per man-hour output for wage earners in manufacturing 2.1 per cent per year, 1870 to 1950, compared to an annual average of 1.3 per cent per year for the same period measured in man-year output per worker.[6] The conclusion then is that the growth rates in GVA (1935-9 prices) per worker shown in column 5 of Table II-4 understate the actual increase when the labour force input has been standardized for changes in hours worked per week.

We assumed, in explaining the changing age-sex structure of the labour force, that skill needs have increased through time, especially in recent decades. The labour input used in Table II-3 contains no such adjustment factor. Since we can also assume that labour quality has increased,[7] then a given unit of labour today with today's technology will probably out-produce a unit of yesterday's lower quality labour. Thus we are probably underestimating the growth in productivity per unit of labour input.

Taking this into account, let us examine the growth in labour productivity. With the exception of the last period, 1929-56, the rate of growth of per capita output exceeded that of output per worker, and it did so for the period as a whole. This result follows, given the earlier discovery that by 1956 the labour force participation ratio was greater than it had been in 1890, implying that, on the average, labour force had grown more rapidly than population. Note also that the trend in per capita output follows a "U" pattern, with high rates of growth occurring in the first and last periods. Per worker trend is entirely different, remaining constant for the first two periods and then accelerating quite substantially in the last (Table II-3, col 5). The constant labour productivity figure for the period 1890 to 1929 is puzzling. Part of the explanation lies in the relationship between the much higher growth in labour force than population over these years (col 2). However, a fuller investigation of the other factors affecting labour productivity must be made before a complete explanation is at hand.

The changes in total labour force and its age-sex restructuring over the 66-year period permit us to relate the denominator of the productivity ratio to its numerator. First, the relationship between the growth of the labour force and the growth of total output is cause-effect. The expansion of output is a signal that job opportunities are opening up in a given labour market area, hence there is an increased demand for labour and an influx of labour from outside or an entry of formerly local non-labour force participants into the labour force. These factors increase the growth of labour force relative to population, and at the same time this labour force growth contributes to output in the economy, thus accelerating its growth. With higher labour participation ratios, the dependency ratio has decreased, and therefore per capita output growth accelerates. Part of the explanation for the very high rate of per capita growth between 1890 and 1910 is probably the rapidly growing labour force. Second, the changes (Table II-3) in the age-sex participation rates, particularly in recent decades, can be said to have had a positive influence on productivity.[8]

SPATIAL DISTRIBUTION OF ECONOMIC ACTIVITY, 1890-1956

*Total GVA*

Our main concern throughout this study is to relate the spatial redistribution of economic activity to national development. One of the first steps in such an investigation is to study the changes in total output among the provinces as they occurred over the 66 years. Table II-4 presents such a picture (a full explanation of the method used to construct these estimates and their biases appears in appendix B). One way to analyse these internal shifts is to divide the 66 years into two basic periods: frontier settlement, 1890 to 1910, and maturity phase, 1910 to 1956. It was observed earlier (Table II-1) that total output expanded rapidly during the first period and showed a variable trend (slower from 1910 to 1929, then more rapid from 1929 to 1956) during the last phase.

An index of total output displacement is shown in line 12, columns 5-9. This index was calculated by summing, disregarding signs, the interperiod shifts of the provincial shares of gross value added. Its meaning is simple: the displacement measure indicates the amount of interprovincial redistribution (here of total output) necessary, at the end date of a given period, to restore the distribution existing in the initial period. This displacement index leads us to conclude that the amount of interprovincial shifting has been large. For example, column 8, line 12, indicates that over 40 per cent of the provincial output in 1956 would have to be reshuffled in order to restore the distribution of 1890, and that this displacement of output was highest in the frontier phase and has steadily declined ever since (note the index calculated on an annual basis, line 14, cols 5-7).

Are these displacement trends in total output in any way associated with variations in the growth of national output? The answer is mixed. In the first period (1890-1910) there is obviously a very close and positive association between frontier expansion and the growth of national output. However, for the balance of the years (1910-56) the association is less obvious. In the period

# TABLE II-4

Distribution and displacement of total GVA in 1935-9 prices, by provinces, selected years, 1890-1956

| | 1890 (1) | 1910 (2) | 1929 (3) | 1956 (4) | Displacement | | | | |
|---|---|---|---|---|---|---|---|---|---|
| | | | | | 1890-1910 (5) | 1910-1929 (6) | 1929-1956 (7) | 1890-1956 (8) | 1910-1956 (9) |
| 1. Canada ($ million) | 1,277 | 2,774 | 5,169 | 14,901 | | | | | |
| 2. P.E.I. | 1.8 | 0.8 | 0.4 | 0.4 | — 1.0 | —0.4 | 0.0 | — 1.4 | —0.4 |
| 3. Nova Scotia | 8.1 | 5.6 | 3.5 | 3.3 | —2.5 | —2.1 | —0.2 | — 4.8 | —2.3 |
| 4. New Brunswick | 6.2 | 3.7 | 2.3 | 2.4 | —2.5 | —1.4 | +0.1 | — 3.8 | —1.3 |
| 5. Quebec | 26.3 | 23.2 | 26.0 | 25.9 | —3.1 | +2.8 | —0.1 | — 0.4 | +2.7 |
| 6. Ontario | 49.3 | 41.4 | 39.3 | 39.2 | —7.9 | —2.1 | —0.1 | —10.1 | —2.2 |
| 7. Manitoba | 3.8 | 6.5 | 6.2 | 4.8 | +2.7 | —0.3 | —1.4 | + 1.0 | —1.7 |
| 8. Saskatchewan | 1.2 | 5.9 | 6.7 | 5.5 | +9.5 | +0.8 | —1.2 | +12.3 | —0.4 |
| 9. Alberta | — | 4.8 | 6.7 | 8.0 | { | +1.9 | +1.3 | { | +3.2 |
| 10. British Columbia | 3.3 | 8.1 | 8.9 | 10.6 | +4.8 | +0.8 | +1.7 | + 7.3 | +2.5 |
| 11. Total per cent | 100.0 | 100.0 | 100.0 | 100.0 | | | | | |
| 12. Total disregarding signs 2-10 | | | | | 34.0 | 12.6 | 6.1 | 41.1 | 16.7 |
| 13. | | | | | 34.0 | 12.6 | 3.7 | 41.1 | 15.9 |
| 14. | | | | | 1.7 | 0.7 | 0.2 | 0.6 | 0.4 |

NOTE: In this and following tables, data for the Yukon and Northwest Territories are included with Saskatchewan and Alberta for this year, thus inflating the estimates of this region. Owing to the insufficient data, the Yukon and Northwest Territories have not been included in the estimates for 1910, 1929, and 1956.

SOURCE AND METHOD: Line 1: GVA for Canada, see appendix B; col 5: col 2 less col 1; col 6: col 3 less col 2; col 7: col 4 less col 3; col 8: col 4 less col 1; col 9: col 4 less col 2; line 12: total displacement, signs disregarded; line 13: total displacement (signs disregarded) adjusted to include 8 provinces for each of the four years. This adjustment was made to eliminate variations between the periods caused by differences in the number of units (e.g., only 8 provinces are shown for 1890, but 9 are included for 1910, 1929, and 1956). A similar calculation was made for Tables II-5 and II-7; line 14: line 12 divided by the number of years in each period.

immediately following the close of the frontier both total national output and the displacement index dropped sharply, but in the last period (1929-56) national output rose sharply, while the displacement index continued to drop. The general conclusion, therefore, is that the relationship between internal redistribution of output and the rate of growth of national product has been declining, and this implies that recent spurts in national growth have been the result of changes in growth patterns within, rather than shifts between, existing provincial production units.

In the actual provincial changes shown in Table II-4, the most important development over the 66-year period was the joining of the western provinces into a full productive partnership with the older eastern provinces. The speed of their growth is no less spectacular: in 1890 the western provinces accounted for about 8 per cent of Canada's total output, by 1910 25 percent, and they more or less held this share through until 1956 (29 per cent) (lines 7-10, cols 1, 2, and 3 of Table II-4). These percentages show again how much vitality the frontier phase added to Canadian growth. Columns 5-9 and lines 1-10 give us another picture of provincial changes in total output, calculated by subtracting the share of total output accounted for by a particular province from the same province's share at the terminal date of the period. If the difference is positive then it indicates that the particular area unit has grown (here in total output) faster than national output, if negative slower, and if zero at the national rate.

From these shift calculations it is observed that, as suspected by now, the main cause of the strong upward spurt of national growth between 1890 and 1910 was the high growth rate experienced by the western provinces during this period (note the large pluses shown in column 5, lines 7-10). What is even of more interest is the convergence in growth rates of total output of all provinces in the period 1910-29. Slower national growth, then, was the joint result of reduced expansion in all provinces, not just a cutback in the growth of the western provinces. The last period presents a more mixed package, but generally there is further convergence towards the national growth rate. These shift findings suggest that, over the whole period to a limited extent, but mainly since 1910, national fortunes have been closely tied to the changes in the growth rates of all provinces: national growth has not been, nor is it now, the outcome of changes in one or two provinces but rather is due to changes in all provinces. We are, in essence, studying the component parts of a unified system. Had we found the opposite condition—where one or two provinces grew at rates above or below the national level while the rest grew continuously at the national level—then the concept of interdependence among these area units would have come into question.

*Population – Total and Age-Sex Structure*
In discussing national population growth we saw that its annual rate has steadily

fallen since the frontier period. How has the spatial distribution of population changed in relation to the national trend in population growth? Table II-5 gives us a view of these provincial population patterns. This table was constructed exactly as was Table II-4 and shows (lines 12-14) the total displacement trends in population as well as the provincial distribution of population at each of the four dates and the shift statistics between periods.

Concentrating on the trends in the displacement index (line 12, cols 5-9) we see that the total shift (line 12, col 9) is almost as great as that for total output (Table II-4, line 12, col 9). The Canadian economy, then, experienced a substantial redistribution in the geographical location of its population during this 66-year period. The trend in the displacement index, like that for total output, has also been steadily down over the three periods (note the annual displacement figures line 14, cols 5, 6, and 7). However, the association between national population growth trends and the regional displacement index path is positively associated in all three periods; both show a consistent decline between the first and last periods. Rapid population growth went with large-scale population reallocation. This strong association was accomplished mainly through heavy immigration rather than by an expansion in domestic population resulting from a rise in natural increase. In the period of Canadian economic development reviewed here, only the years between 1890 and 1910 can be said to have experienced a simultaneous rapid expansion in population and output, thereafter this model requires some modification.

The spatial distribution of the population, as measured in an east-west sense, was largely set in place by 1910, and only minor changes in total displacement occurred subsequently. This does not imply that interprovincial migration has declined, only that the main features of the Canadian population landscape had been set by 1910. The role of the frontier phase of Canadian development comes through clearly when we observe the shift relationships shown in column 5, lines 8-10. It was the strong upward shift in population growth west of Ontario that provided the main impetus to total population growth in Canada. Note also that, as in the case of total output, with slower national population growth there was a convergence in provincial population rates towards this national rate; a convergence which is evident in both the eastern and western provinces. However, the last period is somewhat unlike that for total output. Between 1929 and 1956 the population displacement index declined, but only slightly, implying that although provincial output growth was conforming more closely to the national growth rate, interprovincial population shifts were still playing an important role in national development: in the first period *both* output and population were shifting, but in the last it was population which was adjusting to provincial output differentials. Presumably population was moving towards higher average income regions.

# TABLE II-5

Distribution and displacement of population, by provinces, selected years, 1891-1956

| | 1891 | 1911 | 1929 | 1956 | Displacement | | | | |
| | | | | | 1891-1911 | 1911-1929 | 1929-1956 | 1891-1956 | 1911-1956 |
| | (1) | (2) | (3) | (4) | (5) | (6) | (7) | (8) | (9) |
|---|---|---|---|---|---|---|---|---|---|
| 1. Canada (millions) | 4.8 | 7.2 | 10.0 | 15.6 | | | | | |
| 2. P.E.I. | 2.3 | 1.3 | 0.9 | 0.6 | − 1.0 | −0.4 | −0.3 | − 1.7 | −0.7 |
| 3. Nova Scotia | 9.3 | 6.9 | 5.1 | 4.4 | − 2.4 | −1.8 | −0.7 | − 4.9 | −2.5 |
| 4. New Brunswick | 6.6 | 4.9 | 4.0 | 3.5 | − 1.7 | −0.9 | −0.5 | − 3.1 | −1.4 |
| 5. Quebec | 30.8 | 27.9 | 27.7 | 29.6 | − 2.9 | −0.2 | +1.9 | − 1.2 | +1.7 |
| 6. Ontario | 43.7 | 35.2 | 33.3 | 34.7 | − 8.5 | −1.9 | +1.4 | − 9.0 | −0.5 |
| 7. Manitoba | 3.2 | 6.4 | 6.8 | 5.4 | + 3.2 | +0.4 | −1.4 | + 2.2 | −1.0 |
| 8. Saskatchewan | 2.0 | 6.8 | 8.8 | 5.6 | +10.0 | +2.0 | −3.2 | +10.8 | −1.2 |
| 9. Alberta | — | 5.2 | 6.8 | 7.2 | } | +1.6 | +0.4 | | +2.0 |
| 10. British Columbia | 2.0 | 5.4 | 6.6 | 8.9 | + 3.4 | +1.2 | +2.3 | + 6.9 | +3.5 |
| 11. Total per cent | 100.0 | 100.0 | 100.0 | 100.0 | | | | | |
| 12. Total disregarding signs 2-10 | | | | | 33.1 | 10.4 | 12.1 | 39.8 | 14.5 |
| 13. | | | | | 33.1 | 10.4 | 11.3 | 39.8 | 14.5 |
| 14. | | | | | 1.7 | 0.6 | 0.4 | 0.6 | 0.3 |

NOTE: For Alberta and Saskatchewan figures see first note to Table II-4.

SOURCE AND METHOD: Line 1: population data for 1891 and 1911 from *Census of Canada, 1931*, vol 1, 388-419 and for 1929 and 1956 from the respective *Canada Year Book*; col 5: col 2 less col 1; col6: col 3 less col 2; col 7: col 4 less col 3; col 8: col 4 less col 2; col 9: col 4 less col 2; line 12: total displacement, signs disregarded; line 13: see line 13 of Table II-4; line 14: row 12 divided by the number of years in each period.

Such large population shifts, and particularly shifts in such a short period of time (e.g. 1890 to 1910) would lead one to suspect that in the provinces the age and possibly the sex structure of the population would change. These displacements, as mentioned above, were largely accomplished by internal and external migration, and as a result we might expect a substantial shake-up in population structure over that which would be observed in a closed population environment. This shake-up is due to the age-sex selectivity exhibited by all migration, both internal and external. Thus we would expect the empty regions which receive large population inflows to have a younger population structure than the out-migration or non-immigrant regions in the country.

Table II-6 was constructed to test the structural implications of large-scale population displacement. Two measures of population inequality were derived. The first (lines 1-4) was calculated by subtracting the provincial shares of a given age-sex cohort from the national share of this cohort and summing the resulting deviations, disregarding signs ($\triangle$). The second measure (lines 6-8) weights these deviations by the province's share in total population ($\triangle_w$).[9]

Although both the weighted and unweighted indexes are useful measures of structural inequality (their difference tells us what role the large versus the small provinces are playing in extending or narrowing regional inequality), we shall concentrate our attention on $\triangle_w$ (lines 5-8) in order to minimize the influence of different provincial population sizes on the index. Looking first at inequality levels, it is evident that there are substantial differences between age groups. In particular, for both males and females, $\triangle_w$ is persistently greater for the 0-9 and 25-64 cohorts than for the other age groups. At this stage one can only speculate as to why these particular age groups show greater levels of regional inequality. However, given the impact on regional age structure of migration, it appears that the 25-64 age group must contain an important share of the total movers both to Canada and within Canada. The high index for both sex groups and for the 0-9 group indicates that we are probably observing a family type migration. This is an important area of concern, for the structure of the mover group influences both production and consumption patterns in the receiving and the sending areas.

Turning to the long-term trends in $\triangle_w$, an interesting inequality profile emerges. $\triangle_w$ appears to follow an inverted U path. That is, between 1891 and 1911, regional inequality widens in practically all age groups, persists at this higher level until 1931, and then returns to the previous level by 1951. One interesting exception to this particular profile is the female 25-64 age bracket, which exhibits wider inequality in 1951 than in 1891. The explanation for these variations in $\triangle_w$ lies in the pattern of internal redistribution of the population. We saw earlier that a large reallocation of the population occurred between the 1891 and 1911 period of frontier settlement, but thereafter the index of displacement declined. The co-existence of large internal redistribution with heavy immigration obviously upset regional population structures, and the resulting in-

# TABLE II-6

Changes in the structure of population: percentage distribution of the Canadian population by age and sex, unweighted and weighted absolute deviations of provincial per cents from the Canadian per cent, 1891, 1911, 1931, and 1951

| | Males | | | | | Females | | | | |
|---|---|---|---|---|---|---|---|---|---|---|
| | 0-9 (1) | 10-14 (2) | 15-24 (3) | 25-64 (4) | 65+ (5) | 0-9 (6) | 10-14 (7) | 15-24 (8) | 25-64 (9) | 65+ (10) |
| *Unweighted absolute deviation of provincial per cents from Canadian per cent* | | | | | | | | | | |
| 1. 1891 | 2.6 | 1.6 | 0.8 | 4.8 | 1.4 | 2.6 | 0.4 | 0.8 | 1.7 | 1.4 |
| 2. 1911 | 2.5 | 1.7 | 0.7 | 5.4 | 2.1 | 3.0 | 0.6 | 0.5 | 2.9 | 2.3 |
| 3. 1931 | 2.1 | 0.9 | 0.8 | 4.2 | 1.6 | 2.1 | 1.0 | 1.1 | 3.4 | 1.9 |
| 4. 1951 | 2.0 | 0.9 | 0.7 | 2.7 | 1.3 | 1.9 | 1.0 | 0.8 | 3.1 | 1.3 |
| *Weighted absolute deviation of provincial per cents from Canadian per cent* | | | | | | | | | | |
| 5. 1891 | 2.2 | 0.4 | 0.7 | 2.4 | 0.3 | 2.2 | 0.1 | 0.9 | 1.3 | 0.4 |
| 6. 1911 | 3.1 | 1.2 | 0.5 | 4.7 | 1.2 | 3.3 | 0.7 | 0.2 | 3.5 | 1.2 |
| 7. 1931 | 2.6 | 0.9 | 0.8 | 3.7 | 1.2 | 2.6 | 1.0 | 1.2 | 3.8 | 1.4 |
| 8. 1951 | 2.3 | 0.9 | 0.8 | 2.7 | 1.3 | 2.1 | 0.9 | 1.1 | 2.8 | 1.5 |
| *Per cent of Canadian population* | | | | | | | | | | |
| 9. 1891 | 24.8 | 11.5 | 20.4 | 38.5 | 4.7 | 25.0 | 11.5 | 20.9 | 38.1 | 4.5 |
| 10. 1911 | 22.2 | 9.4 | 19.4 | 44.5 | 4.5 | 24.5 | 10.2 | 19.3 | 41.1 | 4.9 |
| 11. 1931 | 20.8 | 10.1 | 18.4 | 45.2 | 5.5 | 21.8 | 10.6 | 19.2 | 42.7 | 5.6 |
| 12. 1951 | 22.3 | 8.1 | 15.1 | 46.7 | 7.8 | 21.9 | 8.0 | 15.5 | 46.9 | 7.8 |

SOURCE AND METHOD: Appendix Table A-1. Lines 1-4 are the sums, disregarding signs, of the provincial deviations of population shares from their respective national averages, divided by the number of provinces. Lines 5-8 are the sum of the deviations, disregarding signs, of lines 1-4, weighted by the provincial shares in total population.

equalities took several decades to be smoothed out. An interesting conjecture as to why high regional inequality persisted from 1911 to 1931 (or longer?) might be that as annual average immigration declined in the interwar period, internal migration increased. However, the exact relationship between internal and external migration still remains undetermined.

*Labour Force and Labour Participation Ratios*

In the preceding dicussion it was suggested, and partially verified, that migration is age-sex selective, since it was assumed that the major reason for population movement is basically economic: people move towards areas where they expect to realize a net gain on life-time earnings. As such the displacement of popula· tion is really a shift of the labour force from one region or country to another. Also, because this movement is selective, we might expect proportionately more labour to relocate than population. The volume and direction of this movement is our concern in this section.

Table II-7 shows the percentage distribution of the labour force among the provinces and also indicates labour force shifts and the extent of interperiod displacement. The method of construction is identical to that for total gross value added and population. Three main conclusions can be drawn from the table. First, the extent of total labour force displacement over the whole 66-year period is slightly less than for population (compare col 8 in Tables II-5 and II-7). The smaller total displacement for labour force is the joint result of a larger displacement between 1891 and 1911 than for population and smaller shifts subsequently. Note also that the trend in the displacement index (line 14 of Table II-7) is steadily downward, exactly like that for population. The trend in this displacement index is, like that for population, positively associated with the trend in national growth of total labour force. Second, like the areal distribution of total output and population, the large displacement of the first period was the result of frontier settlement in the western provinces; in 1891 these provinces contained approximately 8 per cent of the total Canadian labour force and this climbed to 28 per cent by 1911, holding fairly steady at this level through to 1956 when it was 27 per cent. Third, a look at labour force shifts between provinces (col 5-9, lines 1-10 of Table II-7) indicates the same type of regional growth differentials. The high growth area in the first period was the west. Comparing the shifts to this area we should note that the labour force move into the frontier area is slightly greater than the population shift (compare lines 8-10 in Tables II-5 and II-7). In this connection note the impact on the maritime provinces of frontier expansion. The downward shift in the labour force, as recorded by the shift statistic, exceeded that of population (compare lines 2-4, col 5 in Tables II-5 and II-7). Subsequent provincial shifts show a convergence towards the national labour force growth rate.

One other factor, the relationship between provinces which exhibit labour

TABLE II-7

Distribution and displacement of the labour force, by provinces, selected years, 1891-1956

| | 1891 (1) | 1911 (2) | 1929 (3) | 1956 (4) | Displacement | | | | |
|---|---|---|---|---|---|---|---|---|---|
| | | | | | 1891-1911 (5) | 1911-1929 (6) | 1929-1956 (7) | 1891-1956 (8) | 1911-1956 (9) |
| 1. Canada (millions) | 1.6 | 2.7 | 4.1 | 5.7 | | | | | |
| 2. P.E.I. | 2.2 | 1.2 | 0.8 | 0.6 | — 1.0 | —0.4 | —0.2 | — 1.6 | —0.6 |
| 3. Nova Scotia | 9.8 | 6.4 | 4.8 | 4.2 | — 3.4 | —1.6 | —0.6 | — 5.6 | —2.2 |
| 4. New Brunswick | 6.7 | 4.4 | 3.5 | 3.1 | — 2.3 | —0.9 | —0.4 | — 3.6 | —1.3 |
| 5. Quebec | 28.2 | 24.0 | 26.3 | 27.9 | — 4.2 | +2.3 | +1.6 | — 0.3 | +3.9 |
| 6. Ontario | 45.4 | 36.4 | 34.6 | 37.5 | — 9.0 | —1.8 | +2.9 | — 7.9 | +1.1 |
| 7. Manitoba | 3.4 | 6.5 | 6.7 | 5.7 | + 3.1 | +0.2 | —1.0 | + 2.3 | —0.8 |
| 8. Saskatchewan | 1.3 | 7.7 | 8.2 | 5.7 | +12.3 | +0.5 | —2.5 | +11.2 | —2.0 |
| 9. Alberta | — | 5.9 | 7.0 | 6.8 | | +1.1 | —0.2 | | +0.9 |
| 10. British Columbia | 3.0 | 7.6 | 8.2 | 8.4 | + 4.6 | +0.6 | +0.2 | + 5.4 | +0.8 |
| 11. Total per cent | 100.0 | 100.0 | 100.0 | 100.0 | | | | | |
| 12. Total displacement, signs 2-10 | | | | | 39.9 | 9.4 | 9.6 | 37.9 | 13.6 |
| 13. | | | | | 39.9 | 9.4 | 9.6 | 37.9 | 11.8 |
| 14. | | | | | 2.0 | 0.5 | 0.4 | 0.6 | 0.3 |

NOTE: See note to Table II-6.
SOURCE AND METHOD: Line 1: appendix B; col 5: col 2 less col 1; col 6: col 3 less col 2; col 7: col 4 less col 3; col 8: col 4 less col 1; col 9: col 4 less col 2; line 12: total displacement, signs disregarded; line 13: see line 13 of Table II-4; line 14: line 12 divided by the number of years in each period.

force growth rates above the national average and those which exhibit above average rates of growth in total output, should be noted. High rates of growth of total product are indicative of an active and expanding labour market. One would expect labour to be attracted to such areas and repelled from areas where total product is growing less rapidly than the national average, and if we compare the shift statistics for total output and for labour force (lines 2-10, col 5-7 in Tables II-4 and II-7) this hypothesis seems correct. For example, during the first period, plus signs are observed in both of these variables for the western provinces. In the second period, above average rates of growth of total output appear in Quebec, Saskatchewan, Alberta, and British Columbia and so also for labour force. The last period shows above average growth in labour force in Ontario, Quebec, and British Columbia, but only the latter exhibits an expansion in total output greater than the national rate. However, both Ontario and Quebec show growth rates which are not significantly different from the national level. Thus we have no clear reason to reject the hypothesis even for this last and rather mixed period.

To bring the results of population and labour shifts into perspective the age-sex labour force participation ratios were calculated for each province. Since we are primarily concerned with trends in regional inequality over time, an index of provincial deviations about the national ratio was calculated. This index, like that for the age-sex structure of total population, was obtained both on a weighted ($P_w$) and on an unweighted ($P$) basis. The unweighted index ($P$) was calculated by summing, disregarding signs, the provincial deviation from the national average and dividing the result by the number of provinces. The weighted inequality index ($P_w$) simply multiplied the provincial deviations by the provincial shares in total population.[10]

Table II-8 shows these regional indexes. Primary attention will be focused on the level and trends of regional labour force ratio inequalities, for the same reasons as set in the discussion on regional inequalities in the age-sex distribution of total population. From the table we observe that for both males and females the levels of regional inequality differ substantially between age groups (lines 5-8). In the case of males it is the 15-24 and 65+ age groups which diverge the most, while for females it is 15-24 and 25-64 groups. The explanation for these interage cohort differences is not clear. In the case of males 15-24, the $P_w$ index is greater than the $\triangle_w$ (lines 5-8, Table II-6). This would seem to indicate that "movers" form an important share of this age group and create important differences between regions in their participation ratios. However, the same difference ($P_w > \triangle_w$) applies to males 65+, and for females $P_w > \triangle_w$ for the 15-24 age group, while $P_w < \triangle_w$ for the 25-64 cohort. Stating that when the $P_w$ index is greater than the $\triangle_w$ index it indicates a higher proportion of labour force movers per capita is too simple an explanation. Obviously additional variables must be brought into the equation, e.g., the industrial structure of the regions and its effect on the absolute level of labour force participation

# TABLE II-8

Changes in labour force participation rates: ratio of labour force to population by age and sex, unweighted and weighted, absolute deviations of provincial ratios from Canada ratio 1911, 1931, and 1951

| | Male participation rates | | | | Female participation rates | | | |
|---|---|---|---|---|---|---|---|---|
| | 10-14 (1) | 15-24 (2) | 25-64 (3) | 65+ (4) | 10-14 (5) | 15-24 (6) | 25-64 (7) | 65+ (8) |
| *Unweighted absolute deviations of provincial rates from Canadian rate* | | | | | | | | |
| 1. 1891 (1) | — | — | — | — | — | — | — | — |
| 2. 1911 | 1.2 | 3.2 | 0.9 | 7.0 | 0.4 | 3.8 | 1.3 | 0.8 |
| 3. 1931 | 1.5 | 2.7 | 0.5 | 5.8 | 0.2 | 4.5 | 1.8 | 0.6 |
| 4. 1951 | 0.3 | 2.3 | 0.8 | 3.9 | 0.1 | 4.4 | 2.7 | 0.8 |
| *Weighted absolute deviations of provincial rates from Canadian rate* | | | | | | | | |
| 5. 1891 (1) | — | — | | — | — | — | — | — |
| 6. 1911 | 1.2 | 2.0 | 1.0 | 7.6 | 0.6 | 4.5 | 1.4 | 0.6 |
| 7. 1931 | 1.8 | 2.5 | 0.5 | 6.5 | 0.2 | 5.3 | 2.4 | 0.7 |
| 8. 1951 | 0.1 | 2.3 | 1.1 | 3.8 | 0.1 | 5.3 | 3.2 | 0.8 |
| *Canada participation rates (unweighted)* | | | | | | | | |
| 9. 1891 (1) | — | — | | — | — | — | — | — |
| 10. 1911 | 4.0 | 84.0 | 96.6 | 64.1 | 1.9 | 24.7 | 11.3 | 6.0 |
| 11. 1931 | 2.6 | 74.9 | 96.6 | 60.2 | 0.4 | 30.5 | 13.6 | 6.2 |
| 12. 1951 | 1.1 | 73.7 | 93.8 | 39.2 | 0.4 | 38.9 | 19.2 | 4.8 |

NOTE:   (1) A breakdown of labour force by age was not collected in the 1891 census.

SOURCE AND METHOD:   Participation rates are from appendix Table A-3. Lines 1-4 are the sums, disregarding signs, of the provincial deviations of labour force participation rates by age and sex from the national averages, divided by the number of provinces. Lines 5-8 are the sums, disregarding signs, of lines 1-4, weighted by the provincial shares of population.

ratios. We saw, in this last connection, a change in the composition of the age and sex structures of the labour force as the country moved towards a more advanced stage of development. Such a factor might have to be employed on a cross-section basis if we are to explain the real reasons for differential participation ratios between age groups.

Looking now at the trend in the $P_w$ index we find an even more confusing story. First, the trend analysis is limited to three observations, since the 1891 census does not give an age breakdown of the labour force. Second, for the observations we do have at hand there appears to be no clear long-term profile evident in all age groups. Our expectation might be for some overall convergent trend because of the slowdown in interprovincial labour force displacement. However, with the exception of the youngest and oldest age categories for males and the youngest for females, such convergence does not appear. Again we are left with the conclusion that these trends in $P_w$ may be tied to differential structural demands for labour between regions, and that, if a satisfactory explanation is to be had, this relationship between changes in long-term regional labour demand and trends in regional inequality in participation ratios must be examined first.

## LONG-TERM TRENDS IN REGIONAL INEQUALITY

The central finding of the previous discussion on the growth and spatial distribution of output and population is that Canada experienced, during the 66-year period, substantial geographic changes in the location of economic activity: the shift has been towards the western provinces, and the bulk of the reorientation took place between 1890 and 1910. This still leaves open the question of the balance between output shifts and population movements. If the redistribution of the former were matched exactly with the latter then regional income inequality (assuming the existence of such inequality, initially) would have remained unaltered as a result of such changes. However, should population in-movements overrun output growth or out-migration lag behind retarded growth rates in output, then regional inequality would increase. A simple measure of the relationship between shifts in output, population, and labour force can be obtained from Tables II-4, II-5, and II-7. Each of these tables shows the percentage distribution of one of these statistics. Thus, simply by subtracting the regional shares of population and labour force from the relevant regional share of output, a weighted measure of the regional deviation of per capita and per worker output, respectively, from the national average for each of these averages can be obtained.[11] A negative sign indicates that the particular region's average is less than the national average; a plus sign indicates a level greater than the national. If the output and population or labour force shares are identical, then the province is equal to the national average. As we observe the changes in these deviations between successive periods, an increase in regional deviation indicates a divergence away from the national average, while a decreased deviation a convergence towards the countrywide mean. These deviations also provide us with another measure–total regional inequality. This is obtained by summing, disregarding signs, the regional deviations. An increase in this total between periods indicates a move towards greater regional inequality; a reduction means a move towards regional parity.

Studying line 10 of Table II-9, which shows the changes in secular trends in regional inequality ($\triangle R_w$), we note that the inequity between regions observed in chapter one is not a unique occurrence. Differences between regions in their average level of performance, both in per capita and per worker terms, have persisted since 1890 at least. In addition the level of total inequality has varied over the 66-year period. A pronounced widening is observed between 1890 and 1910. The greater regional inequality continued at this higher level until 1929 and then, for both measures, narrowed. Caution should be exercised in ascribing undue significance to the timing of these changes in divergence and convergence. More complete data (e.g., measures of regional income by decades or quinquennial periods) are required before precise timing is possible. However, these four observations do show that regional inequality is not a recent phenomenon–in fact the level in 1956 is about the same as in 1890–and that variations in inequality over time have occurred.[12]

While discussing the trends in $R_w$, it is worth observing the association between the direction of the trend towards wider or narrower differences and the rate of national growth. A quick look at changes in $R_w$ between 1890 and 1956 indicates a mixed association between regional trends in inequality and national growth. In the two high national growth periods we observe an increase in differences between provinces in the first period, while a narrowing is evident in the last. The middle period shows slower national growth coupled with only slight changes in regional inequality. A simple conclusion that rapid national growth is the best cure for reducing regional differences is far from obvious.[13] The relationship between national growth and regional participation is still undetermined and is potentially a very fruitful area of study.

In addition to showing trends in regional output inequality, Table II-9 sets out the relative provincial ranking in per capita and per worker terms. The most outstanding conclusion from this share difference calculation is the basic constancy of the relative positions of the provinces. From start to finish the maritime provinces and Quebec have average incomes less than the national average; Ontario and British Columbia are persistently higher than the overall average; the prairie provinces exhibit a mixed average hovering near the national level, sometimes above, sometimes below. This ranking stability is quite remarkable given the great changes in the Canadian economy since 1890. Neither frontier settlement (1890 to 1910) nor the gradual maturing of the Canadian economy have significantly altered the positioning of regions within Canada. In the case of the maritime provinces, rapid national growth has brought different reactions:

## TABLE II-9

Sums (disregarding signs) of deviations of shares of population and labour force from shares of GVA in 1935-9 prices, for provinces, selected years, 1890-1956

| | Deviations of GVA from population shares | | | | Deviations of GVA from labour force shares | | | |
|---|---|---|---|---|---|---|---|---|
| | 1890 (1) | 1910 (2) | 1929 (3) | 1956 (4) | 1890 (5) | 1910 (6) | 1929 (7) | 1956 (8) |
| 1. | −0.5 | −0.5 | −0.5 | −0.2 | −0.4 | −0.4 | −0.4 | −0.2 |
| 2. | −1.2 | −1.3 | −1.6 | −1.1 | −1.7 | −0.8 | −1.3 | −0.9 |
| 3. N... | −0.4 | −1.2 | −1.7 | −1.1 | −0.5 | −0.7 | −1.2 | −0.7 |
| 4. Quebec | −4.5 | −4.7 | −1.7 | −3.7 | −1.9 | −0.8 | −0.3 | −2.0 |
| 5. Ontario | +5.6 | +6.2 | +6.0 | +4.5 | +3.9 | +5.0 | +4.7 | +1.7 |
| 6. Manitoba | +0.6 | +0.1 | −0.6 | −0.6 | +0.4 | 0.0 | −0.5 | −0.9 |
| 7. Saskatchewan | −0.8 | −0.9 | −2.1 | −0.1 | −0.1 | −1.8 | −1.5 | −0.2 |
| 8. Alberta | (¹) | −0.4 | −0.1 | +0.8 | (¹) | −1.1 | −0.3 | +1.2 |
| 9. British Columbia | | +2.7 | +2.3 | +1.7 | +0.3 | +0.5 | +0.7 | +2.2 |
| 10. Total 1-9 (disregarding signs) | | 18.0 | 16.6 | 13.8 | 9.2 | 11.1 | 10.9 | 10.0 |

NOTE: (1) The Yukon and Northwest Te[rritories] ... included with Saskatchewan and Alberta for this year.

SOURCE AND METHOD: See Tables II-4, II-5, an... ...rces. Col 1: col 1 of Table II-4 less col 1 of Table II-5; col 2: col 2 of Table II-4 less col 1 of Table II-4 less ...f Table II-5; col 3: col 3 of Table II-4 less co... ...II-5; col 4: col 4 of Table II-4 less col 4 of Table II-5; col 5: col 1 of Table II-4 less ...r Table II-7; col 6: col 2 of Table II-4 less col ...-7; col 7: col 3 of Table II-4 less col 3 of Table II-7; col 8: col 4 of Table II-4 less col 4 of Table II-4 ... of Table II-7.

between 1890 and 1910, rapid expansion brought decreased participation to this area, while from 1929 to 1956 increased participation. But one thing does stand out clearly: the slow growth from 1910 to 1929 widened the differences between these provinces and the rest of the country. In addition, in spite of its high degree of industrialization coupled with its locational advantages, Quebec has remained consistently below the national average and below that of its neighbour, Ontario. Why this divergence in Quebec and why its persistence are still largely unsolved mysteries. The below average level of educational attainment of the labour force and the more rural, lower productivity agricultural sector pointed up in the cross-section study of chapter one might serve as introductory areas of investigation to the Quebec "problem."

The last observation from Table II-9 is the lower level of total regional inequality exhibited by the per worker measure (line 10, cols 5-8), which adjusts provincial averages for differences in labour force per capita. In chapter one we saw that such an adjustment reduced the level of regional inequality. It does so again here. In spite of this adjustment, however, the trend ($\triangle R_w$) towards wider provincial differences between 1890 and 1910 followed by a narrowing (slight) in the last period persists. Also, the adjustment for participation ratios does not seriously alter the relative ranking of provinces.

# 3
# Regional Inequality and Structural Change, Selected Periods, 1890-1956

BETWEEN 1890 and 1956 the share of workers engaged in the A sector (agriculture, forestry, fishing, and trapping) declined from 53 to 24 per cent. Such a drastic reallocation of labour is clear testimony to the joint impact of productivity changes in the A sector, permitting the release of labour without a decrease in total production and differential income elasticity of demand between A and non-A sector products. Initial shares of workers engaged in these resource industries exceeded the national averages in some provinces, while in others were less, and in some provinces over the 66-year period subsequent declines substantially diverged from the national record. This chapter consists of an investigation of the relationship between regional income growth and the accompanying change in labour and output composition. The following questions will be considered: What influence did shifts in labour force between sectors and provinces and changes in output per worker within sectors and provinces exert on period changes in *countrywide* and provincial productivity? What relationship exists between long-term trends in regional inequality in average and per worker output and national economic growth? Does the existence of an expansive national economic area affect regional interaction? The answers to these questions will indicate the impact that different determinants of regional growth have exerted on the structure of the subnational units' development and, simultaneously, present a preliminary explanation of why average levels of performance among these units have differed.

The previous chapter on the long-term trends in national and regional growth provided a clue to the extent of spatial reallocation which has accompanied Canadian development since 1890. In particular, the period of frontier settlement before the first world war initiated an important change in the regional sources of national growth. The variations in provincial participation in this expansive phase of development and during the subsequent decades implied that we were studying an integrated system of subnational units. However, the nature of the link between regions could not be fully ascertained by observing trends in the growth of aggregate output and input. The ties obviously arose from the structural interaction between these units, i.e., in a demand-supply context. It is this consilience of differential regional needs and the capacity to meet them through structural transformation that is the central concern in what follows.

INTER- AND INTRASECTORAL CHANGES IN PRODUCT PER WORKER

To measure the extent of the interprovincial structural changes that have accompanied developments in Canada over the 66-year period, Table III-1 was constructed. It allocates changes in per worker output, to the influences caused by shifts in the composition of output and those resulting from variation in productivity. In other words Table III-1 assigns, for each of the three time intervals, the addition to per worker gross value added, in constant prices, countrywide (line 2), to: changes in GVA per worker within sectors, and effects of shifts in weights of sectors within the countrywide total of labour force (lines 3 and 4); changes in GVA per worker *within* provinces, and effects of shifts in weights of provinces within the countrywide total of labour force (lines 6 and 7); or changes in GVA per worker within sector-province-cells, and effects of shifts of sector-province-cells within the countrywide total of labour force (lines 9 and 10). In each case the method of deriving the *intra* change is to allow *per worker product within the sector*, or province, or cell, to move over the interval but to hold the *weights* (shares) of sector, province, cell, etc., in countrywide labour force constant. The method of deriving the *inter* change is to allow the *weights* (shares), in countrywide labour force of the sectors, or provinces, or cells to move, and to hold the *per worker* GVA *within* the sector, province, or cell, constant over the interval.

From Table III-1 we can conclude: (1) the contribution of intersectoral shifts to the rise in countrywide GVA per worker throughout is small; (2) that the interprovincial shifts were greatest during the period of frontier expansion, while after 1911 the relative importance of these shifts declined sharply and continuously; (3) that the contribution of intercell shifts, being dominated by interprovincial shifts, is a direct result of conclusion (2). The small contribution of shifts in labour force among sectors (line 4) tends to conform with one of Denison's findings.[1] However, conclusion (2) indicates that redistribution of the labour force among provinces has played an important role. This relationship can be brought out more clearly by comparing the amount of redistribution of labour force among provinces between 1890 and 1911 (Table II-7) with the contribution of interprovincial changes in the first period (line 7, Table III-1). Also, after 1911 a sharp and continuous decline occurs in both the amount of labour force displacement among provinces (Table II-7) and the contribution of interprovincial shifts to the total change in per worker product (line 7, Table III-1). The small amount of labour force displacement in the last period shows how important changes in output per worker *within* sectors and provinces are to the total change in output per worker, since, in spite of a sharply diminished amount

# TABLE III-1

Intra- and intersectoral changes in product per worker in constant 1935-9 dollars, between provinces, sectors, and the interaction of provinces and sectors for selected periods, 1890-1956

| | GVA per worker 1890 (1) | GVA per worker 1910 (2) | 1890-1910 Percentage distribution (3) | 1910-29 GVA per worker (1929) (4) | 1910-29 Percentage distribution (5) | 1929-56 GVA per worker (1956) (6) | 1929-56 Percentage distribution (7) |
|---|---|---|---|---|---|---|---|
| 1. GVA per worker in constant (1935-9) dollars | 800.33 | 1,018.16 | | 1,255.86 | | 2,601.19 | |
| 2. Total change in (1) | | 217.83 | | 237.70 | | 1,345.33 | |
| 3. Intrasectoral change | | 228.42 | 100.00 | 233.68 | 99.00 | 1,335.17 | 98.83 |
| 4. Intersectoral change | | −11.37 | — | 2.36 | 1.00 | 15.87 | 1.17 |
| 5. Total (3) and (4) | | 217.05 | 100.00 | 236.04 | 100.00 | 1,351.04 | 100.00 |
| 6. Intraprovincial change | | 135.49 | 62.87 | 181.67 | 77.42 | 1,190.70 | 88.26 |
| 7. Interprovincial change | | 80.03 | 37.13 | 53.00 | 22.58 | 158.36 | 11.74 |
| 8. Total (6) and (7) | | 215.52 | 100.00 | 234.67 | 100.00 | 1,439.06 | 100.00 |
| 9. Intracell change | | 141.97 | 65.63 | 174.73 | 74.41 | 1,192.11 | 88.20 |
| 10. Intercell change | | 74.34 | 34.37 | 60.09 | 25.59 | 159.46 | 11.80 |
| 11. Total (9) and (10) | | 216.31 | 100.00 | 234.82 | 100.00 | 1,351.57 | 100.00 |

SOURCE AND METHOD: Line 1: see Table II-4; lines 3-11: industrial distribution of the labour force, 1891, *Census of Canada, 1891*, vol II, 140; 1911-51, *Census of Canada, 1951*, vol IV, Table 2. Extrapolations from the 1931 and 1951 census to 1929 and 1956 were made on the basis of indices of provincial employment (by sectors) changes which appear annually in the *Canada Year Book*. Lines 3, 6, and 9: calculated by multiplying the average labour force shares for the particular period by the GVA (1935-9 prices) per worker for the initial and terminal years and calculating the difference. Lines 4, 7, and 10: calculated by multiplying the average GVA (1935-9 prices) per worker for the period by the respective labour force shares for the initial and terminal years and subtracting the initial year's results from the terminal results.

of interprovincial redistribution, the greatest increase in product per worker occurs between 1929 and 1956 (Table III-1, line 2).

TRENDS IN REGIONAL PER CAPITA AND WORKER OUTPUT INEQUALITY

The first step in the analysis of the causes behind the growing divergence in per worker product (first outlined in Table II-10 and associated with the open frontier period of Canadian development) is to examine the trends in the un-weighted and weighted absolute and relative deviations of GVA per capita (Table III-2). Regional inequality can be measured in weighted or unweighted or in

---

TABLE III-2

Changes in total GVA (1935-9 prices) per capita: unweighted and weighted absolute and relative deviations of provincial levels from Canada level, 1890, 1910, 1929, and 1956

|  | 1890 | 1910 | 1929 | 1956 |
|---|---|---|---|---|
|  | (1) | (2) | (3) | (4) |
| 1. Unweighted absolute deviation of provincial GVA per capita from Canadian level | 55.75 | 74.00 | 115.44 | 167.56 |
| 2. Unweighted relative deviation from Canadian level | 0.20 | 0.20 | 0.26 | 0.19 |
| 3. Canada total GVA per capita | 283 | 365 | 450 | 861 |
| 4. Weighted absolute deviation from Canadian level | 38.46 | 67.91 | 102.69 | 144.03 |
| 5. Weighted relative deviation from Canadian level | 0.14 | 0.19 | 0.23 | 0.17 |

SOURCE AND METHOD:　Cols 1-4: line 1 represents the sum, disregarding signs, of the provincial deviations of GVA per capita from the national average. Basic data are shown in appendixes B and C. Line 2 is the ratio of line 1 to line 3. Line 3 is the unweighted national average, i.e.,

$$\frac{i = \sum_{1}^{9} \left(\frac{Y}{P}\right)_i}{n}, \text{ where } \left(\frac{Y}{P}\right)_i = \text{average output per capita in the } i\text{th province, and } n = \text{the}$$

total number of provinces. Line 4 represents the sum, disregarding signs, of the provincial deviations of GVA per capita from the national average, weighted by the provincial distribution of population (relative to Canada total) Table II-5. Line 5 is the ratio of line 4 to line 3.

absolute or relative terms. The weighted *relative* deviations are used in this analysis, because the unweighted absolute deviations suffer from two limitations. First, the latter are strongly influenced by the erratic behaviour of small subnational units. For example, a province in the early stages of development, when its population share in the total is small, may have this small number of people concentrated in some specific pursuit (e.g., agriculture, mining, etc.) and rely on imports to satisfy the balance of its needs. However, as the population grows, this concentration in one or two activities becomes impractical, and its economic base diversifies. In studying the trends in interprovincial differences in per capita product, we may find a narrowing tendency in differentials arising for no other reason than the growth of small subnational units. To avoid this influence on our discussion of convergence or divergence in this and subsequent series, the unweighted deviations were multiplied by appropriate weights (in this case by provincial distribution of total population), and the weighted deviations, disregarding signs, were totalled (line 4). Note, that for all years under study the weighted absolute deviations are less than unweighted figures, which indicates that on balance the smaller provinces, for these years, have the larger deviations. Also, with weighting, the problem of consistency when shifting from eight provinces in 1890 to nine for the balance of the study is overcome. The second limitation in using simple absolute deviations (weighted or unweighted) arises from the influence of the change, at the national level, in the size of the components. Thus, if a certain series under study represents only a small percentage of the national total, we would expect its subnational share to be very small and its degree of divergence at any date to be insignificant. To avoid this problem, the total deviations (unweighted and weighted) were divided by the national average of the components under study (line 3).

Table III-2 reveals the persistent increase in both the unweighted and weighted absolute deviations of per capita product from the early to the later years; we should also note that the largest divergences occur in the later periods. The implication is that the poor regions have grown at slower rates, in average terms, than the richer ones. Even to have maintained the absolute difference over the 66-year period, the poorer provinces would have had to grow at rates much greater than the richer regions. The failure of the former to do so implies their growth rates were probably closer, on average, to the national rate. A move towards convergence in the last period, however, can be observed in the unweighted and weighted *relative* measures (lines 2 and 5). Before 1929 only the weighted relatives showed a consistent move towards divergence among the provinces, which implies that, up to 1929, the larger provinces were experiencing larger deviations than the smaller ones.

To be more specific, the increasing disparity between provinces between 1890 and 1910 was caused mainly by the improvement in the relative levels of per capita output of Ontario and British Columbia. Both these provinces were above the national average in 1890 and both, obviously, were the main beneficiaries of western settlement. Between 1910 and 1929 the largest changes in levels occurred in the maritime provinces, Ontario, Quebec, Alberta, and British Columbia. The maritimes diverged downward from the national average, while the other four provinces substantially increased their relative positions above the countrywide average. In the last period, with the return of above average national growth rates, almost all of the total change occurred as a result of the sharp upward shift in the relative positions of Ontario, Alberta, and British Columbia.

The first step in analysing the factors contributing to these trends in regional inequality in GVA per capita is to see the effect exerted by variations in the ratio of total labour force to total population. Table III-3 presents these data, calculated in a method similar to that outlined for Table III-2. From Table III-3 we can conclude that both the unweighted and weighted absolute and relative deviations decrease from 1891 to 1951, which indicates a growing convergence, over time, in the share of labour force in population in the subnational units, towards the national pattern and hence among the subnational units themselves. The other important point is that this convergence did not begin until after 1911.[2] This delay in the movement towards convergence may, as stated in chapter two, have been caused by the heavy immigration into Canada which occurred in the first two decades of this century. The influence of this mass inflow was to distort the participation rates upward in the receiving areas (prairie provinces and British Columbia) relative to the older more settled regions. With the reduction in this flow after the mid-1920s, plus a reduction in migration to the former frontier areas, the population age and sex structures converged to the national pattern (Table II-6), and participation rates tended to conform to those of the national average. Evidence of the convergence, it might be added, occurs even when the provinces are weighted by their shares in total population (line 3, Table III-3).

TABLE III–3

Changes in labour force participation rates: ratio of total labour force to total population, unweighted and weighted absolute and relative deviations of provincial ratios from Canada ratio, 1891, 1911, 1931, and 1951

|  | 1891 (1) | 1911 (2) | 1931 (3) | 1951 (4) |
|---|---|---|---|---|
| 1. Unweighted absolute deviation of provincial participation rate from Canadian rate | 4.4 | 4.8 | 2.3 | 1.9 |
| 2. Unweighted relative deviation from Canadian rate | 0.12 | 0.12 | 0.06 | 0.05 |
| 3. Weighted absolute deviation from Canadian rate | 3.6 | 3.7 | 2.0 | 2.2 |
| 4. Weighted relative deviation from Canadian rate | 0.10 | 0.09 | 0.05 | 0.06 |

SOURCE AND METHOD: Participation rates are from appendix Table A-3. Cols 1-4: line 1 represents the sum, disregarding signs, of the provincial deviations of participation rates from the national average; line 2 is the ratio of line 1 to the unweighted national average at each date. See method Table III-2. Line 3 represents the sum, disregarding signs, of the provincial deviations of labour force participation rates from the national average, weighted by the provincial distribution of total population (relative to Canadian total). Line 4 is the ratio of line 3 to the unweighted national average at each date (see method Table III-2).

Part of the explanation for the convergence in per capita GVA (1935-9 prices) relatives after 1929 can be traced to the growing similarity in the relation of labour force to population among the provinces. Had we discovered that over time certain provinces were receiving abnormally large shares of the young and old compared to other regions, then we would have expected a growing divergence in per capita product resulting from the differences between the regions in the number working (i.e., where the labour force relative to total population is greater, then total income is larger than where the rate is lower, and so we would assume that per capita product is greater in the former than the latter). This, indeed, is what we observed between 1890 and 1910. After 1929 we would suppose that the growing conformity among the subnational units in their share of labour force in total population would, over time, be a moderating influence on inequalities in per capita product.

Turning now to the trend in deviations of GVA per worker (Table III-4), we observe that they are the same as observed in Table III-2 for GVA per capita.[3] That is, the divergences increase over the whole period in the weighted and unweighted absolute deviations, especially between 1890 and 1910.[4] The opening of the frontier and rapid settlement provided the impetus (for the years covered here) for a steady upward trend in absolute deviation, and, as in the case of GVA per capita, the poorer provinces experienced growth rates substantially less than the rich regions. Only a detailed study of the poorer provinces will indicate the causes of the modification in their growth rates. When the relatives (lines 2 and 5) are observed, however, a tendency towards convergence among the subnational units after 1929 is seen. These per worker relatives follow closely the

TABLE III-4

Changes in total GVA (1935-9 prices) per worker: unweighted and weighted absolute and relative deviations of provincial levels from Canada level, 1890, 1910, 1929, and 1956

|  | 1890 (1) | 1910 (2) | 1929 (3) | 1956 (4) |
|---|---|---|---|---|
| 1. Unweighted absolute deviation of provincial GVA per worker from Canadian level | 85.63 | 126.22 | 208.78 | 446.11 |
| 2. Unweighted relative deviation from Canadian level | 0.11 | 0.14 | 0.19 | 0.19 |
| 3. Canada total GVA per worker | 773 | 920 | 1,090 | 2,401 |
| 4. Weighted absolute deviation from Canadian level | 75.70 | 144.71 | 217.31 | 299.27 |
| 5. Weighted relative deviation from Canadian level | 0.10 | 0.16 | 0.20 | 0.12 |

SOURCE AND METHOD: Cols 1-4: line 1 represents the sum, disregarding signs, of the provincial deviations of GVA per worker from the national average; line 2 is the ratio of line 1 to line 3; line 3 is the unweighted average of GVA per worker; line 4 represents the sum, disregarding signs, of the provincial deviations of GVA per worker from the national average, weighted by the provincial distribution of total labour force (relative to Canada total). See Table II-7. Line 5 is the ratio of line 4 to line 3.

trends exhibited by GVA per capita (Table III-2). A pattern in regional inequality appears to be emerging: a divergence away from the national average starting with western settlement followed by a convergence since the late 1920s. The exact dating of these trend changes should be treated with caution. What is important is the fact that a long swing in regional inequality took place. The implication is that regional growth rates were altered during the early decades of the twentieth century, and that it took several decades to restore regional inequality to its initial level.

A check of the provinces mainly responsible for these trends in GVA per worker shows that, on the whole, they are the same as those contributing to trend changes in GVA per capita. However, Quebec plays a more prominent role, especially in the first two periods. For example, in per worker terms Quebec showed a marked increase in its relative position from below the national average in 1890 to a position well above in 1910. However, when the output of the province was divided by total population, as in Table III-2, its relative position below the national average in 1890 remained practically unchanged over this period. One would want to look very closely in the case of Quebec into the relationship between total population change (natural increase plus the balance of net migration) and the growth of total output. Did, for example, Quebec fail to participate in western settlement to the extent of Ontario and the maritimes? One indication that the answer here is in the affirmative is that between 1891 and 1911 Quebec's labour force per capita ratios diverged away from the national average (indicating increased dependence levels), while Ontario's ratio converged sharply towards the countrywide level, being initially below. If lower out-migration from Quebec was the case, the important question of why the difference remains unanswered–cultural factors, economic causes?

Another interesting difference between trends in per capita and per worker inequality is in their levels (compare lines 5 in Tables III-2 and III-4): the per worker relatives are consistently lower. The conclusion, supported by the cross-sectional evidence in chapter one (see the discussion surrounding Table I-5), is that a substantial amount of total regional inequality is caused by provincial differences in labour force per capita. From this we could infer that one way the poorer provinces can reduce the income gap is to encourage greater labour force participation.

TREND CHANGES IN REGIONAL GVA AND LABOUR FORCE STRUCTURE

The next logical step in analysing the factors contributing to long-term regional inequality is to examine the structural differences in industrial output and labour force among the provinces. By collecting data in the form of gross value added a breakdown of this total by sectoral contribution is possible. The measurement technique applied to these sectoral breakdowns is identical to that employed in measuring regional inequality in average and per worker GVA. Table III-5 shows

TABLE III-5

Changes in structure of labour force: percentage distribution of the Canadian labour force by industrial components, unweighted and weighted absolute and relative deviations of provincial per cents from the Canadian per cent, 1890, 1910, 1929, and 1956

| | A sector | Mining and manufacturing | S sector plus construction | Total |
|---|---|---|---|---|
| | (1) | (2) | (3) | (4) |
| *Unweighted absolute devia-tion of provincial per cents from Canadian per cent* | | | | |
| 1. 1890 | 9.01 | 6.19 | 3.04 | 18.24 |
| 2. 1910 | 11.72 | 7.42 | 6.72 | 25.87 |
| 3. 1929 | 12.07 | 7.00 | 6.22 | 25.29 |
| 4. 1956 | 10.00 | 7.31 | 3.93 | 21.24 |
| *Weighted absolute deviation of provincial per cents from Canadian per cent* | | | | |
| 5. 1890 | 5.40 | 3.95 | 1.64 | 10.99 |
| 6. 1910 | 11.03 | 7.84 | 4.61 | 23.48 |
| 7. 1929 | 14.23 | 8.84 | 6.05 | 29.12 |
| 8. 1956 | 10.88 | 10.04 | 2.41 | 23.33 |
| *Per cent of Canadian labour force* | | | | |
| 9. 1890 | 52.5 | 16.4 | 31.0 | 100.0 |
| 10. 1910 | 43.3 | 16.2 | 40.4 | 100.0 |
| 11. 1929 | 41.2 | 15.5 | 43.2 | 100.0 |
| 12. 1956 | 24.0 | 20.2 | 55.8 | 100.0 |
| *Unweighted relative devia-tion from Canadian per cent* | | | | |
| 13. 1890 | 0.17 | 0.38 | 0.10 | 0.18 |
| 14. 1910 | 0.27 | 0.46 | 0.17 | 0.26 |
| 15. 1929 | 0.29 | 0.45 | 0.14 | 0.25 |
| 16. 1956 | 0.42 | 0.36 | 0.07 | 0.21 |
| *Weighted relative deviation from Canadian per cent* | | | | |
| 17. 1890 | 0.10 | 0.24 | 0.05 | 0.11 |
| 18. 1910 | 0.25 | 0.48 | 0.11 | 0.23 |
| 19. 1929 | 0.35 | 0.57 | 0.14 | 0.29 |
| 20. 1956 | 0.45 | 0.50 | 0.04 | 0.23 |

NOTE:   A sector is comprised of agriculture, forestry, and fishing and trapping; S sector is comprised of transportation, domestic commerce, and other services (personal and professional); construction was included with the S sector to reduce its currently, unexplained erratic behaviour.

SOURCE AND METHOD:   Lines 9-12: see Table II-7 for sources of provincial distributions of labour force. Cols 1-3: lines 1-4 are the sums, disregarding signs, of the provincial deviations these inequality indices. Our main concern is with the trends of the weighted relative deviations. This particular measure is important because it takes account not only of the changes in the size of subnational units over time– the weighting by the distribution of total labour force among provinces–but also of the shifts in size of each component in the national total. For example, between 1890 and 1956, the share of labour force in the A sector dropped from 53 to 24 per cent. By dividing the weighted absolute deviations by their respective national shares, the effect of a change in share sizes is eliminated.

We start this analysis of changing structural inequality with a look at trend changes in labour force shares between provinces, or at the geographical shifts in an important input component. Although our main concern is with the weighted relatives, it will be instructive to analyse the changes in all the measures shown in Table III-5 to test for consistency in the direction of movement. The first observation is that the measure of inequality for all sectors combined (col 4) is, *without exception*, larger in 1956 than in 1890. This implies that the distribution of workers between the A sector and mining and manufacturing and the S sector plus construction was, over time, *less similar* to the national distribution of these three components and to each other in 1956 than in 1890. This trend towards divergence, however, was not consistent with the result obtained when we broke the 66-year span into the three subperiods. Concentrating our attention on column 4, lines 17-20 (weighted relative deviations), we see that divergence in structure grew from 1890 to 1929 but narrowed appreciably in the last period (1929-56). Note also, in connection with these weighted relatives, that the largest change upward was between 1890 and 1910.

This discovery of a growing dissimilarity between regions over time is interesting in the light of our findings in chapter two of the vast internal redistribution of population and labour force that took place between 1890 and 1956. Add to this the changing distribution between agricultural and non-agricultural workers (lines 9-12), which, other things being equal, would favour an approach to greater similarity in the structure among subnational units, and it seems reasonable to have expected an overall convergence in structure. Also of interest is the fact that the main shift towards divergence in structure came in the period of greatest population growth and internal migration (1890 to 1910). Thus, it appears especially in connection with the last point, that the decades of vast immigration and frontier expansion were not conducive to greater structural similarity among provinces but, in fact, contributed to regional specialization.

Which of the three sectors under study, then, was of most importance in

---

of labour force shares from the national share, divided by the number of provinces; lines 5-8 are the sum of the deviations obtained in lines 1-4, disregarding sign, weighted by the provincial distribution of total labour force; lines 13-20 are the ratios of lines 1-8 divided by lines 9-12.

causing the trend towards structural inequality in the labour force? Studying primarily the weighted relatives (lines 17-20), we see that both the A sector and mining and manufacturing inequality indexes increased considerably between 1890 and 1956, suggesting that the distribution among provinces of workers in these groups has become more concentrated. Also, this move towards concentration occurred within the context of decreasing shares of the A sector in the total labour force and increasing shares of mining and manufacturing. The former, with its decreasing shares and increasing concentration, is approximately what we would have expected, while the latter, increasing shares and increasing concentration, is not. Thus, if a sector is increasing its share of total output, it seems reasonable to assume that the activity would gradually become more widely diffused, in a geographic sense. The finding of the opposite trend in Table III-5 for mining and especially for manufacturing, which dominates this sector, implies a substantial structural rigidity through time in the composition of production between provinces.

These findings on trends in regional inequality beg the question of which provinces were the gainers and which the losers in specific types of economic activity. In the case of the A sector, for the first period Saskatchewan was the principal gainer in labour force, while Ontario, Quebec, and British Columbia all witnessed sharp reductions in their shares below the national average. The increasing concentration of agricultural activity in the prairies, which largely continued over the last two periods, is what we would expect given the nature of the westward population movements. A completely different shift occurred in the mining and manufacturing sector, where Ontario and Quebec were the principal gainers. The biggest increase in the concentration of mining and manufacturing in the central provinces occurred between 1890 and 1910. However, these two provinces continued to increase their relative positions for the last two periods as well. Thus part of the explanation for the structural rigidity in this sector mentioned earlier can be explained by the early and persistent dominance of Ontario and Quebec in secondary manufacturing activity and mining.

Trends and levels of regional inequality for the S sector plus construction are substantially different from the other two sectors. The S sector constitutes a series of products which, in the main, are not sold at any great distance from the origin of their production. High transportation costs prohibit extensive long-distance trade. The proof of this is clearly evident in the low level of inequality indexes for this sector (lines 17-20, col 3 of Table III-5). A low absolute level of this index indicates that production is widely diffused among the provinces. Thus, regardless of the level of income, each province requires a certain minimum level of output from this sector. The other two sectors can concentrate production and sell over a wider area (note their larger inequality indexes). A glance at the trends in the inequality index for this sector shows a very mixed pattern, compared with trend indexes for the A and mining and manufacturing sectors. For example, the S sector plus construction was the only component to show a marked convergence in its inequality index in the last period. Like the other sectors, however, it did show a tendency towards greater regional concentration between 1890 and 1911, with this trend continuing until 1929. In the first period, British Columbia was the most important single contributor to the rise in the index, undoubtedly a reflection of the role of shipper and provider of trading services to the west. In the second period Ontario and Quebec were the largest gainers in labour force working in this sector. After 1910, British Columbia no longer can be considered the leading contributor to the growth in the index of inequality for this sector.

The influence of the S sector plus construction reversed itself in the last period with both the weighted absolute and relative deviations declining. This decrease in disparity was the result, primarily, of a shift in the shares of Quebec and Ontario *towards* the national average. This trend towards similarity in shares of the S sector in labour force among the provinces coupled with its growing share in the total labour force was the cause of the reduction in the overall weighted relative, outlined earlier (line 20, col 4).

To investigate further these structural changes between subnational units, the unweighted and weighted absolute and relative deviations for GVA (1935-9 prices) were calculated (Table III-6). A study of the overall trends in the totals of these measures reveals a growing dissimilarity in structure as in the case of the structural distribution of the labour force. The data reveal that all measures, observing totals (col 4), show an increase between 1890 and 1956; the period of greatest increase in structural divergence occurs between 1890 and 1910; the A sector and mining and manufacturing exhibit a steady increase in their respective weighted relatives; and the S sector plus construction behaves in an erratic fashion, both contributing to and lessening, at different periods, the overall divergent tendency. In fact, not only are the trends the same, but the provinces primarily responsible for these shifts correspond to those outlined in the discussion of changing labour force shares between provinces. The conclusion, then, is that the movement in the shares of GVA over time was towards a growing dissimilarity in structure between the subnational units and the countrywide distributions, and between those subnational units and themselves. But, since the output estimates are constructed from a wide variety of background data, the chance for estimation error is naturally much greater than in the figures on labour force shares by sectors. The closeness of *levels* of inequality by sectors –i.e., much higher for the A and mining and manufacturing sectors than for the S sector plus construction and in trends towards greater regional specialization– lends some support to the belief that the regional output estimates are, at the least, good indicators of changing economic performance among the provinces. Also, the fairly close agreement indicates that labour, through geographic and sectoral mobility, has accommodated itself to the changing structure of demands as they are evidenced in the composition of final output.

TABLE III-6

Changes in structure of GVA (1935-9 prices): percentage distribution of GVA by sectors, un-weighted and weighted absolute and relative deviations of provincial per cents from the Canadian per cent, 1890, 1910, 1929, and 1956

| | A sector (1) | Mining and manufacturing (2) | S sector plus construction (3) | Total (4) |
|---|---|---|---|---|
| *Unweighted absolute deviation of provincial per cents from Canadian per cent* | | | | |
| 1. 1890 | 10.16 | 7.06 | 4.43 | 21.65 |
| 2. 1910 | 11.02 | 9.56 | 5.40 | 25.98 |
| 3. 1929 | 10.77 | 7.82 | 5.21 | 23.80 |
| 4. 1956 | 7.06 | 9.66 | 7.87 | 24.58 |
| *Weighted absolute deviation of provincial per cents from Canadian per cent* | | | | |
| 5. 1890 | 6.70 | 5.30 | 2.10 | 14.10 |
| 6. 1910 | 9.79 | 10.65 | 3.99 | 24.06 |
| 7. 1929 | 11.21 | 9.72 | 3.48 | 24.41 |
| 8. 1956 | 8.19 | 13.64 | 7.65 | 29.48 |
| *Per cent of Canadian GVA* | | | | |
| 9. 1890 | 40.5 | 21.1 | 38.4 | 100.0 |
| 10. 1910 | 36.6 | 20.7 | 42.7 | 100.0 |
| 11. 1929 | 21.2 | 18.5 | 60.2 | 100.0 |
| 12. 1956 | 15.2 | 24.4 | 60.4 | 100.0 |
| *Unweighted relative deviation from Canadian per cent* | | | | |
| 13. 1890 | 0.25 | 0.34 | 0.11 | 0.22 |
| 14. 1910 | 0.30 | 0.46 | 0.13 | 0.26 |
| 15. 1929 | 0.51 | 0.42 | 0.09 | 0.24 |
| 16. 1956 | 0.46 | 0.40 | 0.13 | 0.25 |
| *Weighted relative deviation from Canadian per cent* | | | | |
| 17. 1890 | 0.17 | 0.25 | 0.05 | 0.14 |
| 18. 1910 | 0.27 | 0.51 | 0.09 | 0.24 |
| 19. 1929 | 0.53 | 0.53 | 0.06 | 0.24 |
| 20. 1956 | 0.54 | 0.56 | 0.12 | 0.29 |

NOTE: For a definition of the A and S sectors see Table III-5.

SOURCE AND METHOD: Lines 9-12: for the provincial distribution of GVA (1935-9 prices) see appendix B. For calculation procedure see Table III-2.

REGIONAL INEQUALITY IN SECTORAL GVA PER WORKER

Table III-7 presents the results of estimating regional inequality trends in sectoral productivity, where productivity is output, by sector, per unit of un-

TABLE III-7

Changes in the structure of sectoral GVA (1935-9 prices) per worker: GVA per worker by sectors, unweighted and weighted absolute and relative deviations of provincial GVA per worker from Canadian GVA per worker, 1890, 1910, 1929, and 1956

| | GVA per worker | | |
|---|---|---|---|
| | A sector (1) | Mining and manufacturing (2) | S sector plus construction (3) |
| *Unweighted absolute deviations of provincial levels from Canadian level* | | | |
| 1. 1890 | 122.00 | 176.25 | 51.50 |
| 2. 1910 | 143.11 | 287.44 | 50.11 |
| 3. 1929 | 125.78 | 269.56 | 180.44 |
| 4. 1956 | 664.78 | 1,165.89 | 244.56 |
| *Weighted absolute deviation of provincial levels from Canadian level* | | | |
| 5. 1890 | 108.82 | 71.84 | 55.62 |
| 6. 1910 | 155.77 | 299.05 | 53.73 |
| 7. 1929 | 115.34 | 219.49 | 142.93 |
| 8. 1956 | 525.30 | 635.23 | 157.90 |
| *Canada GVA per worker* | | | |
| 9. 1890 | 600 | 1,046 | 950 |
| 10. 1910 | 772 | 1,140 | 980 |
| 11. 1929 | 518 | 1,340 | 1,510 |
| 12. 1956 | 1,595 | 3,104 | 2,520 |
| *Unweighted relative deviation from Canadia level* | | | |
| 13. 1890 | 0.20 | 0.17 | 0.05 |
| 14. 1910 | 0.19 | 0.25 | 0.05 |
| 15. 1929 | 0.24 | 0.20 | 0.12 |
| 16. 1956 | 0.42 | 0.38 | 0.10 |
| *Weighted relative deviation from Canadian level* | | | |
| 17. 1890 | 0.18 | 0.07 | 0.06 |
| 18. 1910 | 0.20 | 0.26 | 0.05 |
| 19. 1929 | 0.22 | 0.16 | 0.09 |
| 20. 1956 | 0.33 | 0.20 | 0.06 |

NOTE:   For a definition of the A and S sectors see Table III-5.
SOURCE AND METHOD:   For basic data consult Tables III-5 and III-6. Cols 1-3: see Table III-2 for method of calculation.

adjusted labour input used in its respective output. The method of calculating the absolute (weighted and unweighted and relative) deviations is identical with that employed in Table III-4, but total output is disaggregated into the three sectors shown (cols 1-3).

Turning first to the trend in the A sector, we find an increase in inequality for all four measures between 1890 and 1956 (col 1). Two periods are particularly prominent: 1890 to 1910, and 1929 to 1956. In the case of the former, three provinces contributed the major share of this divergence (measured in terms of weighted absolute deviations): Ontario, Manitoba, and British Columbia, all moving from a position above the national average in 1890 to one even greater in 1910. With respect to the last period (1929-56) there were two opposite trends contributing to divergence in GVA per worker between provinces in this sector. In the first the maritime provinces, Quebec, and Ontario shifted to a position well below the national average, a trend already in progress by 1929, since the five provinces were below the countrywide average at this date. On the other hand, British Columbia, which held a position above the national average in 1929, diverged sharply upward in the last period.

The mining and manufacturing sector, like the A sector, increased in divergence between provinces in levels of GVA per worker between 1890 and 1956. In the first period the provinces contributing most to this divergence were Quebec, Ontario, British Columbia, and Saskatchewan; the first three improved their already favourable positions above the countrywide average, while Saskatchewan declined even further behind this average. In the last period the growth in inequality in levels of output per worker was a combination of an increase in the relative positions of Ontario, Saskatchewan, Alberta, and British Columbia coupled with a decline in the position of the maritime provinces. Both these trends were continuations of established positions in 1929.

The S sector plus construction, although exhibiting a trend towards greater divergence between 1890 and 1956, arrived at this final position by a different time pattern than that observed for the other two sectors. In this case the major increase in inequality came between 1910 and 1929 (col 3). Examining the movement in weighted absolute deviations between these two dates, we find that the maritime provinces, Ontario, Alberta, and British Columbia were the main contributors to this shift. For the maritimes it was a case of falling even further behind the countrywide average, while for the remaining provinces the change was to a position of greater positive weighted deviations than for 1910.

Concentrating now on the relative index of inequality (lines 17-20), we observe that for the A and mining and manufacturing sectors the overall trend is towards a greater dissimilarity among provinces in output per worker, while for the S sector plus construction no persistent long-term trend is evident. In the case of the first two sectors this pattern (towards greater inequality) corresponds to the pattern observed for shares of labour force and output; another similarity is that the levels of inequality are greater in the A sector and mining and manufacturing than for the S sector. Splicing these trend results with our knowledge of the main provincial gainers in shares and productivity indicates that these two events begin to converge: greater sectoral specialization in a region brings greater productivity levels. Added support for this position appears in the inequality indexes measured in absolute terms (lines 1-8), which show very high levels of inequality in 1956 as compared to 1890. The implication is that the poorer provinces' output per worker has grown at considerably slower rates than in the richer provinces, especially for the mining and manufacturing sector. Structural rigidity in the form of substantial regional inequalities in the shares of sectoral output appears to be an important factor contributing to provincial inequality.

# 4
# Explanations of Trends in Regional Inequality

THE EXISTENCE of regional inequality in Canada has been documented in the previous chapters. A quick review reveals two outstanding aspects of the process of economic growth in Canada between 1890 and 1956. The first is the persistence over the 66-year period of regional inequalities in average output. By 1956, the weighted dispersion of output per capita was about the same as it was in 1890. Also, with a few exceptions, the provinces with the highest average output in 1890 still had the highest in 1956 and those with the lowest continued, throughout, to hold that unenviable honour. The second is the variation in regional inequality over the period; although provincial positions on the income scale were relatively fixed, differentials between the top provinces and the bottom first widened and then narrowed. In particular a divergence in average output was observed between 1890 and 1910, followed by a period of relatively high level inequality and then a tendency towards convergence after 1929.

This description of trends in regional inequality leaves us without any explanation of them. It also fails to integrate the variations in geographic distribution of sectoral output and labour shares with the general pattern of average and per worker inequality. Towards an explanation of our observations the inverted U hypothesis provides an interesting framework within which to discuss the major sources in the movement of regional inequality. At the end of the chapter a brief discussion on the applicability of the staple hypothesis in explaining the observed differential rates of total provincial growth will be made.

In setting out to explain variations in income inequality we are concerned with two basic variables: the share of provincial total output in national output, and the provincial shares in population (and labour force). A study of the changing sizes of these two measures between provinces obviously involves consideration of the principal elements which determine economic change. Since all variables are shifting it will be impossible, with our limited range of data, to pinpoint the exact causes of changes or to successfully predict how the two will interact. The explanations offered here are merely presented as tentative approaches to the performance of regions during the process of national development.

INVERTED U HYPOTHESIS

The inverted U hypothesis states that in the course of national development variations in regional inequality occur. The concept that shifts in regional income shares are not matched precisely with movements of population is an extension, into a spatial context, of a hypothesis put forward by Simon Kuznets, who used changing income inequality among households rather than among regions.[1] In his outline, widening income inequality was attributed to the shifting of population (and labour force) from rural to urban sectors. Inequality was increased when he assumed that the size distribution of income among households was more unequal in an urban setting than in a rural one. This was held to be a temporary condition limited mainly to the period of an economy's transition to an industrial society. Time eventually smoothed out the distribution, and a shift towards equality occurred at later stages.

The analogy between changing regional inequality and variations in the size distribution of income among households is not direct but can serve as a starting point. To begin with, it divides the past into subperiods: the first is one of increasing inequality; the second a period of high level inequality; the third a shift towards greater equality among the units. In the regional case, the first stage (widening inequality) would coincide with a reallocation in the distribution of total output and population among provincial units. Since provinces or regions generally have divergent levels of per capita and per worker output, then shifting weights of population shares, assuming relative levels of performance remain approximately the same, will mean changes in total inequality. Considerable time might pass before adjustment towards a more even balance between income and population shares is accomplished. The two later stages represent this process of the gradual elimination of the higher levels of inequality. Since the interrelationship of income and population growth is still largely unknown, the sequence of events outlined makes no pretence of explaining how changes in income operate on the population or vice versa. It is simply a framework which states that at certain stages in the development process regional fortunes change, and that the resulting shifts in income and population distributions tend to increase regional inequality. Finally, because of market imperfection, considerable time (possibly several decades) is required to restore the initial level of inequality.

The Kuznets model indicates, in addition to the time profile of inequality, that greater inequality is consistent with "the early stages of economic growth when the transition from the pre-industrial to the industrial civilization was most rapid."[2] The task, then, is to pinpoint the period of transition and offer some explanation of the forces initiating it. Since the inverted U hypothesis partitions long-term development into specific phases, the 66-year period was divided into a frontier phase (1890 to 1910), and an urban-industrial phase (1910 to 1956). The former is meant to cover the main period of prairie settlement, while the latter roughly embraces the gradual transition of the economy from a rural-resource orientation to an urban-manufacturing focus.[3]

FRONTIER PHASE, 1890-1910

The basic characteristic of this phase of national development is territorial expansion, accomplished by the movement of capital and labour to areas where land is abundant and cheap; settlement generally proceeds rapidly.[4] The question is: Can the exploitation of western lands satisfactorily explain the observed widening in regional income inequality (Table III-2 shows that GVA per capita increased from 0.14 to 0.19)? It was observed that one cause of the widening phase in inequality was the transition of the economy from a rural-farming to an urban-industrial society. Here, however, we seek to explain the impact of a shift of resources from developed to undeveloped regions.

The traditional explanation of the expansion in total output and population and the accompanying internal redistribution during the period 1890 to 1910 is wheat exploitation: "Wheat was not merely the largest export and product of the new region, it was the central dynamic and unifying force of the expansion."[5] It is our task to explain why such population and output redistribution should increase regional inequality. The first step is to recall (Table II-9) that between 1890 and 1910 most of the increase was the result of shifts in the relative positions of Ontario and British Columbia (upward) and Saskatchewan and Alberta (downward). How can the observed population displacements be tied in with these changes? The prairie provinces' average and per worker output levels declined during this 20-year period from slightly above the national average to below by 1910. Given the greatly increased share of total population residing in the west by 1910, the result was to increase total weighted inequality. In British Columbia the opposite conditions prevailed: population flowed into a region that enjoyed levels of performance above the national average. The result in this latter case was to add to total inequality through a greater weight by an upward divergent province. Ontario's case is different again. Although its share in total population declined, the upward expansion in average output, coupled with the province's large absolute size (i.e., 35 per cent of total population in 1910) made this upward shift an important contributor to total inequality. Thus, shifting population weights among provinces, assuming relatively fixed per capita and per worker levels, then, were an important cause of widening inequality.

However, in addition to changing regional weights in total output, we observed (Tables II-4 and II-7) that a substantial change in regional shares of sectoral output and labour input occurred. The main shift was towards greater specialization, with the central provinces greatly expanding their shares of total manufacturing output and the prairies moving to the top in shares of agricultural output (especially Saskatchewan). British Columbia, from the start, had only a small share of its labour force in agriculture. In the central provinces, the intra-provincial shift was towards the M sector and the S sector, which enjoyed above average levels of productivity and a boost in their average level of performance. But Ontario gained, while Quebec did not. The question of why such divergence in spite of a somewhat similar structural shift remains unanswered. In a similar vein the structure of British Columbia's output became even more concentrated in the above-average output sectors, so raising its level further.

The prairies are a contrast. Their primary intraprovincial shifts went towards the agricultural sector. This sector traditionally shows relative levels of performance below countrywide ouput per worker levels. The result was to keep average performance at or below the countrywide level. Thus within a region structural shifts coupled with large population displacements combined to increase regional inequality (a division of the impact of interprovincial versus intraprovincial changes in output per worker is shown in Table III-1).

### URBAN-INDUSTRIAL PHASE, 1910-56

If expansive nationalism plus a changing relationship between regions can be credited with part of the divergence among provinces between 1890 and 1910, what impact did a shift to a more urban-industrial form of development have on the subsequent trends in regional inequality? After 1910 the index of per capita and per worker product widened until 1929, and this was followed by a slight convergence during the last period (Table III-4). In a very general way this time profile corresponds to the second and third stages of the inverted U hypothesis. A brief overview of developments in Canada after 1910 shows that growth during the period 1910 to 1929 was slower than in the preceding years (1890 and 1910), while the last period was one of rapid growth. These 46 years after 1910 embrace the variable growth of the 1920s (slow early in the decade giving way to accelerated expansion towards the end). The following two decades witnessed the depression, with low aggregate demand and large quantities of unemployed resources, followed by maximum utilization of the country's resources during the second world war and a boom in postwar economic activity through to 1956.

Despite this highly varied performance the average annual compound rate of growth in real GVA per capita from 1910 to 1956 was 2.0 (Table II-2). This quite respectable post-1910 national growth was, however, coupled with a substantially different performance in changes of regional shares of output and population than occurred between 1890 and 1910. Tables II-4, lines 5 and 7, show that regional displacement of GVA, population, and labour force dropped sharply and continuously after 1910. This could be expected with the filling-in of the last large open area within the country.

Within this later phase of development there are two distinct subparts: the 1910 to 1929 period when national growth was relatively slow and inequality among provinces continued to increase, and the period from 1929 to 1956 when countrywide growth was higher and regional convergence was observed. Little at this stage can be said about persistently higher levels of regional inequality in the 1910-29 period. A glance at Table II-9 shows that it was primarily a change in the relative positions of the maritime provinces (moving further below the national average), Quebec (a shift upwards), and Saskatchewan (greater divergence below) that contributed to widening inequality. Here the role of population and labour displacement, unlike the frontier period, is much less important (see Table II, lines 5 and 7). More of the burden of explanation, therefore, shifts to intraprovincial changes in output per worker, and for this the evidence is sketchy. In the maritimes, A sector output dropped sharply, but labour shares in this sector only slowly. The main output expansion came in the S sector. Quebec showed substantial expansion in S sector output. Saskatchewan witnessed a large drop in the share of agricultural output not matched by a similar drop in this sector's share of the labour force. With the exception of these changes the general interregional structure remained relatively unchanged. The only conclusion to be drawn is that slower national growth during this period was apparently connected with the observed wider inequality. The exact connection is not known at this time.

In the last period some convergence in per capita and per worker inequality was observed, and one fact does stand out–the sharp change among provinces in their share of population. In the frontier period all the plus signs (indicating growth rates greater than the national average) were for provinces west of Ontario. This general pattern, although much reduced, continued into the second period. However, after 1929 the provinces with above average population increases were Ontario, Quebec, Alberta, and British Columbia (Table II-5), indicating that now population was moving towards provinces, with the exception of Quebec, with average levels of performance exceeding the national average and out of provinces of below average per capita and per worker product.[6] The result of this shift in migration streams towards higher income, more industrialized regions has been to lower the divergence in per worker income. Thus more of the total population is residing in above average income regions. The effect of this redirection of migration is shown by the convergence in per worker and per capita output towards the national average for all provinces, except Quebec (which diverges away from the countrywide mean) and Alberta (which shifts upwards). The most notable convergence is in per worker output in the maritime provinces. Recent shifts in the sources of national economic growth, then, from a frontier-agricultural focus to an urban-industrial pattern of development appear to have influenced the trend of regional inequality.

STAPLE THEORY

The preceding discussion on trend variations in regional inequality has been devoid, with the minor exception of detailing some of the changes in levels of national economic performance, of any specific discussion of the determinants of regional growth (total or average), because the topic of regional growth determinants is much too large to be undertaken within the framework of this study. However, it might be worthwhile to make a few remarks on the general applicability of the staple thesis in explaining some of the broad changes in the pattern of Canadian regional development observed since 1890.

The staple model seeks an explanation to the determinants of economic growth in a resource rich, population scarce economy.[7] Growth in such a case proceeds by attracting to the region the necessary factors of production–capital and labour–which can only be attracted to the new region by increasing earnings relative to the old region (characterized as one where resources are scarce but plentiful in labour and capital). The discovery of some high-quality natural resource, coupled with a high level of sustained demand for it, is sufficient to encourage exploitation. The rise in demand price is transmitted to factor prices, which then rise relative to those in the older region. As a result factors move to the new region and production commences.

The focus in this model is on the commodity: its discovery, location, quality, and prospective demand. Moreover, the staple model forces us to consider the nature of the production characteristics of the commodity. It is obvious that different staples require different types, quantities, qualities, and mixes of factors, along with different levels of technical apparatus and economic organization. The early users of this staple approach were quite aware of the central role the staple played in explaining developments (see, for example, their comparison of the local impact of cotton production in the southern United States with wheat in the west and, for Canada, the influence of fur exploitation versus lumber). These long-run impacts of staple exploitation have been formalized in discussions of the production function of the staples and the resulting linkages through input requirements and output possibilities in the development of non-resource sectors within the new and older regions.

The problem facing us is: How well does the staple model explain secular trend variations in regional inequality? To begin with it must be emphasized that the staple model cannot predict variations in the average level of performance. This is obvious from the very nature of the model which seeks to explain the movement of both capital and labour into new areas. The rates at which each comes plus the quality of the resources and level of technology are all *variables*. The outcome of *all* these factors will determine levels and secular trends in per capita and per worker output. For the "frontier phase" of development (1890 to 1910), it would appear that the staple model is a good explanatory tool. Rising wheat prices beginning at the end of the nineteenth century were coupled with greatly increased flows of immigrants and foreign capital, plus the large internal reallocation of population and labour force outlined earlier. The result of the latter shifts to areas of agricultural production, we noted, tended to create greater divergence among provinces in average output by increasing the weight in the national total of the below average income provinces. Simultaneous regional specialization in production was observed, which tended to increase the levels of product per worker because of the intraregional shift (mainly in Ontario, Quebec, and British Columbia) towards sectors having higher relative outputs per worker.

When we shift to the later phases of growth, especially the period of convergence (1929 to 1956), the staple model's importance would appear to diminish. If one could demonstrate that staple expansion was primarily responsible for the shift towards regional equity, it would have to be shown either that the new staples are less regionally focused than the earlier ones, or that they are the type which would tend to raise per capita product of the benefitting regions *more* than they would raise the per capita product of other regions and that the benefitting regions might be among the lower income regions. This is difficult to demonstrate, if indeed it did happen. It would appear, however, that during this later phase of growth less emphasis on export of natural resource exports as a growth determinant seems a reasonable presumption, and more emphasis should be placed on the rise of the internal market.[8] The expansion of the latter, especially as it has meant a growth in non-agricultural output, has been focused in the central provinces, Alberta (mining), and British Columbia. It is towards these provinces, as we have shown, that population has moved in recent times.

CONCLUSION

Only the broadest possible implications are warranted from a study such as this, which deals with such long periods and such aggregate data. However, if an answer is sought as to the value of being a region within a national union or an independent nation, the persistence of much lower *intranational* income disparities over long periods than those observed between countries is sufficient to justify membership. Participation in a rapidly growing national union seems to set a floor to performance and keeps income disparity low. These advantages, though, are mixed with some obvious disadvantages. Although *intranational* income disparities are less than *international*, the evidence presented here indicates that membership does not guarantee equal levels of participation for all the subnational units. National economic development is no guarantee of regional income parity. The cost of membership is seen most clearly in the constant relative positions of the different provinces. The poorer provinces remain poor and experience growth rates substantially less than the rich provinces. Reliance simply on national growth to eliminate this gap appears a doubtful solution. If income disparities among the provinces are to be reduced, regional growth problems must take on a large share of our concern in the period ahead.

The nature of this investigation into regional aspects of Canada's economic growth has precluded any precise conclusions on the mechanism which ties national and regional change together. It has merely "blocked out" the general shape of events and shown the magnitudes involved. Important questions remain. For example, the timing of the change in secular trends in regional inequality is important, for a change in trend direction signals a modification of the underlying growth process. If we can pinpoint more accurately the dating of these trend changes (through additional benchmark estimates), it might be possible to understand more fully their causes. Thus, the opening of the frontier obviously was an important event in Canadian economic history both with respect to regional *and* national development. We would like to know precisely how frontier expansion was linked to development of the older regions. In addition, knowledge on when the frontier's influence began to diminish and which variables were affected first is essential to our understanding of subsequent events, especially the convergent trend after 1929.

One of the truly perplexing problems in this study is the persistently lower level of average performance in Quebec than in Ontario. The former province received many of the structural "benefits" of the latter during the frontier phase but did not realize as rapid a rate of expansion–at least not rapid enough to close the income gap between the two. A search for answers to this problem would seem imperative. In addition, further research in regional growth determinants could focus on filling in the obvious statistical gaps, especially the unknown period before 1890, plus adding more recent benchmark estimates, and beginning a systematic investigation of the determinants of regional growth through a disaggregation of sectoral totals.

Appendixes, Notes, and Index

# Population, Labour Force, and Labour Force Participation Rates by Provinces 1891, 1911, 1931, and 1951

TABLE A-1

Population distribution, total and percentage, by age and sex, 1891, 1911, 1931, and 1951 (00 omitted)

| | 1891 | | 1911 | | 1931 | | 1951 | |
|---|---|---|---|---|---|---|---|---|
| | Total | Per cent | Total | Per cent | Total | Per cent | Total | Per cent |

*Prince Edward Island*

MALE

| | | | | | | | | |
|---|---|---|---|---|---|---|---|---|
| 0-9 | 139 | 25.3 | 103 | 21.8 | 95 | 20.9 | 120 | 24.0 |
| 10-14 | 70 | 12.7 | 55 | 11.6 | 48 | 10.6 | 48 | 9.5 |
| 15-24 | 113 | 20.6 | 94 | 19.9 | 85 | 18.7 | 75 | 15.0 |
| 25-64 | 196 | 35.7 | 183 | 38.7 | 182 | 40.0 | 211 | 42.0 |
| 65+ | 31 | 5.6 | 38 | 8.0 | 45 | 9.8 | 48 | 9.6 |
| 10+ | 412 | 74.7 | 370 | 78.2 | 360 | 79.1 | 382 | 76.0 |
| All ages | 550 | 100.0 | 473 | 100.0 | 455 | 100.0 | 502 | 100.0 |

FEMALE

| | | | | | | | | |
|---|---|---|---|---|---|---|---|---|
| 0-9 | 132 | 24.5 | 99 | 21.1 | 92 | 21.6 | 116 | 24.0 |
| 10-14 | 66 | 12.1 | 51 | 10.8 | 46 | 10.8 | 45 | 9.4 |
| 15-24 | 110 | 20.4 | 93 | 20.0 | 75 | 17.5 | 73 | 15.3 |
| 25-64 | 203 | 37.5 | 184 | 39.4 | 169 | 40.0 | 199 | 41.3 |
| 65+ | 30 | 5.6 | 41 | 8.6 | 45 | 10.1 | 49 | 10.1 |
| 10+ | 409 | 75.5 | 369 | 78.8 | 335 | 78.4 | 366 | 76.0 |
| All ages | 541 | 100.0 | 468 | 100.0 | 427 | 100.0 | 482 | 100.0 |

*Nova Scotia*

MALE

| | | | | | | | | |
|---|---|---|---|---|---|---|---|---|
| 0-9 | 541 | 23.9 | 579 | 23.1 | 560 | 21.3 | 772 | 23.8 |
| 10-14 | 275 | 12.1 | 263 | 10.5 | 287 | 10.9 | 295 | 9.1 |

TABLE A-1 *(continued)*

| | 1891 Total | 1891 Per cent | 1911 Total | 1911 Per cent | 1931 Total | 1931 Per cent | 1951 Total | 1951 Per cent |
|---|---|---|---|---|---|---|---|---|
| 15-24 | 472 | 20.9 | 475 | 19.0 | 502 | 19.1 | 488 | 15.1 |
| 25-64 | 849 | 37.5 | 1,012 | 40.5 | 1,080 | 41.1 | 1,422 | 43.8 |
| 65+ | 130 | 5.8 | 175 | 7.0 | 203 | 7.6 | 272 | 8.4 |
| 10+ | 1,726 | 76.1 | 1,925 | 76.9 | 2,072 | 78.7 | 2,477 | 76.2 |
| All ages | 2,267 | 100.0 | 2,504 | 100.0 | 2,632 | 100.0 | 3,249 | 100.0 |
| FEMALE | | | | | | | | |
| 0-9 | 522 | 23.4 | 563 | 23.4 | 545 | 21.8 | 741 | 23.3 |
| 10-14 | 261 | 11.7 | 255 | 10.6 | 279 | 11.2 | 286 | 9.0 |
| 15-24 | 460 | 20.7 | 461 | 19.2 | 463 | 18.6 | 490 | 15.5 |
| 25-64 | 853 | 38.2 | 944 | 39.2 | 1,006 | 40.3 | 1,382 | 43.5 |
| 65+ | 135 | 5.1 | 185 | 7.5 | 205 | 8.2 | 277 | 8.7 |
| 10+ | 1,709 | 76.6 | 1,845 | 76.6 | 1,953 | 78.2 | 2,435 | 76.7 |
| All ages | 2,231 | 100.0 | 2,408 | 100.0 | 2,498 | 100.0 | 3,176 | 100.0 |

*New Brunswick*

MALE

| | 1891 Total | 1891 Per cent | 1911 Total | 1911 Per cent | 1931 Total | 1931 Per cent | 1951 Total | 1951 Per cent |
|---|---|---|---|---|---|---|---|---|
| 0-9 | 414 | 25.3 | 436 | 24.3 | 495 | 23.8 | 685 | 26.5 |
| 10-14 | 199 | 12.1 | 196 | 10.9 | 238 | 11.4 | 251 | 9.7 |
| 15-24 | 333 | 20.4 | 342 | 19.1 | 395 | 19.0 | 383 | 14.7 |
| 25-64 | 602 | 36.7 | 709 | 39.4 | 817 | 39.2 | 1,076 | 41.5 |
| 65+ | 88 | 5.4 | 110 | 6.2 | 140 | 6.7 | 196 | 7.5 |
| 10+ | 1,222 | 74.7 | 1,357 | 75.7 | 1,590 | 76.2 | 1,906 | 73.5 |
| All ages | 1,636 | 100.0 | 1,793 | 100.0 | 2,085 | 100.0 | 2,591 | 100.0 |
| FEMALE | | | | | | | | |
| 0-9 | 394 | 25.0 | 426 | 24.8 | 484 | 24.3 | 658 | 25.7 |
| 10-14 | 186 | 11.8 | 187 | 10.9 | 231 | 11.6 | 244 | 9.5 |
| 15-24 | 329 | 20.9 | 333 | 19.4 | 377 | 18.9 | 411 | 16.0 |
| 25-64 | 589 | 37.4 | 668 | 38.9 | 771 | 38.7 | 1,057 | 41.3 |
| 65+ | 76 | 4.8 | 106 | 6.2 | 134 | 6.7 | 194 | 7.6 |
| 10+ | 1,180 | 75.0 | 1,294 | 75.2 | 1,513 | 75.7 | 1,906 | 74.3 |
| All ages | 1,574 | 100.0 | 1,720 | 100.0 | 1,997 | 100.0 | 2,564 | 100.0 |

*Quebec*

MALE

| | 1891 Total | 1891 Per cent | 1911 Total | 1911 Per cent | 1931 Total | 1931 Per cent | 1951 Total | 1951 Per cent |
|---|---|---|---|---|---|---|---|---|
| 0-9 | 2,092 | 28.2 | 2,743 | 27.2 | 3,558 | 24.6 | 5,123 | 25.4 |
| 10-14 | 877 | 11.8 | 1,115 | 11.1 | 1,581 | 10.9 | 1,836 | 9.1 |
| 15-24 | 1,444 | 19.4 | 1,916 | 19.0 | 2,782 | 19.2 | 3,323 | 16.4 |
| 25-64 | 2,656 | 36.0 | 3,844 | 38.1 | 5,861 | 40.6 | 8,805 | 43.6 |
| 65+ | 346 | 4.7 | 456 | 4.5 | 689 | 4.8 | 1,134 | 5.6 |
| 10+ | 5,323 | 71.8 | 7,331 | 72.8 | 10,913 | 75.4 | 15,098 | 74.6 |
| All ages | 7,415 | 100.0 | 10,074 | 100.0 | 14,471 | 100.0 | 20,221 | 100.0 |
| FEMALE | | | | | | | | |
| 0-9 | 2,054 | 27.6 | 2,739 | 27.7 | 3,510 | 24.6 | 4,928 | 24.3 |
| 10-14 | 852 | 11.5 | 1,108 | 11.2 | 1,577 | 11.1 | 1,775 | 8.7 |

TABLE A-1 *(continued)*

| | 1891 | | 1911 | | 1931 | | 1951 | |
|---|---|---|---|---|---|---|---|---|
| | Total | Per cent | Total | Per cent | Total | Per cent | Total | Per cent |
| 15-24 | 1,479 | 20.0 | 1,911 | 19.3 | 2,887 | 20.3 | 3,461 | 17.1 |
| 25-64 | 2,714 | 36.6 | 3,697 | 37.3 | 5,598 | 39.2 | 8,986 | 44.2 |
| 65+ | 328 | 4.4 | 459 | 4.6 | 700 | 4.9 | 1,186 | 5.9 |
| 10+ | 5,373 | 72.4 | 7,175 | 72.3 | 10,762 | 75.4 | 15,408 | 75.7 |
| All ages | 7,427 | 100.0 | 9,914 | 100.0 | 14,272 | 100.0 | 20,336 | 100.0 |

*Ontario*

MALE

| | Total | Per cent | Total | Per cent | Total | Per cent | Total | Per cent |
|---|---|---|---|---|---|---|---|---|
| 0-9 | 2,470 | 23.1 | 2,566 | 19.8 | 3,248 | 18.6 | 4,681 | 20.2 |
| 10-14 | 1,236 | 11.6 | 1,187 | 9.2 | 1,616 | 9.2 | 1,657 | 7.2 |
| 15-24 | 2,236 | 21.0 | 2,507 | 19.4 | 3,110 | 17.8 | 3,371 | 14.6 |
| 25-64 | 4,203 | 39.4 | 5,984 | 46.1 | 8,359 | 47.7 | 11,520 | 49.7 |
| 65+ | 517 | 4.9 | 706 | 5.5 | 1,055 | 6.5 | 1,903 | 8.2 |
| 10+ | 8,192 | 76.9 | 10,384 | 80.2 | 14,140 | 81.4 | 18,451 | 79.8 |
| All ages | 10,662 | 100.0 | 12,950 | 100.0 | 17,388 | 100.0 | 23,132 | 100.0 |

FEMALE

| | Total | Per cent | Total | Per cent | Total | Per cent | Total | Per cent |
|---|---|---|---|---|---|---|---|---|
| 0-9 | 2,394 | 23.0 | 2,500 | 20.4 | 3,157 | 18.8 | 4,459 | 19.5 |
| 10-14 | 1,196 | 11.5 | 1,148 | 9.4 | 1,566 | 9.3 | 1,596 | 7.0 |
| 15-24 | 2,284 | 21.9 | 2,353 | 19.3 | 2,991 | 17.8 | 3,309 | 14.5 |
| 25-64 | 4,096 | 39.4 | 5,530 | 45.2 | 7,918 | 47.2 | 11,368 | 49.8 |
| 65+ | 448 | 4.4 | 707 | 5.8 | 1,205 | 7.1 | 2,101 | 9.2 |
| 10+ | 8,024 | 77.0 | 9,738 | 79.6 | 13,680 | 81.2 | 18,374 | 80.5 |
| All ages | 10,418 | 100.0 | 12,238 | 100.0 | 16,837 | 100.0 | 22,833 | 100.0 |

*Manitoba*

MALE

| | Total | Per cent | Total | Per cent | Total | Per cent | Total | Per cent |
|---|---|---|---|---|---|---|---|---|
| 0-9 | 214 | 26.2 | 579 | 23.2 | 720 | 19.6 | 833 | 21.1 |
| 10-14 | 79 | 9.7 | 220 | 8.8 | 390 | 10.6 | 306 | 7.8 |
| 15-24 | 174 | 21.3 | 508 | 20.4 | 714 | 19.4 | 570 | 14.4 |
| 25-64 | 335 | 41.1 | 1,132 | 45.3 | 1,684 | 45.7 | 1,876 | 47.5 |
| 65+ | 14 | 1.7 | 60 | 2.4 | 174 | 4.7 | 354 | 8.9 |
| 10+ | 602 | 73.8 | 1,920 | 76.8 | 2,962 | 80.4 | 3,106 | 78.9 |
| All ages | 816 | 100.0 | 2,499 | 100.0 | 3,682 | 100.0 | 3,939 | 100.0 |

FEMALE

| | Total | Per cent | Total | Per cent | Total | Per cent | Total | Per cent |
|---|---|---|---|---|---|---|---|---|
| 0-9 | 207 | 31.6 | 568 | 27.4 | 703 | 21.2 | 793 | 20.8 |
| 10-14 | 74 | 11.3 | 214 | 10.4 | 375 | 11.3 | 295 | 7.7 |
| 15-24 | 130 | 19.8 | 424 | 20.5 | 701 | 21.1 | 589 | 15.4 |
| 25-64 | 232 | 35.5 | 814 | 39.3 | 1,397 | 42.2 | 1,839 | 48.2 |
| 65+ | 12 | 1.8 | 50 | 2.4 | 143 | 4.3 | 301 | 7.9 |
| 10+ | 448 | 68.4 | 1,502 | 72.6 | 2,616 | 78.8 | 3,024 | 79.2 |
| All ages | 655 | 100.0 | 2,070 | 100.0 | 3,319 | 100.0 | 3,817 | 100.0 |

*Saskatchewan*

MALE

| | Total | Per cent | Total | Per cent | Total | Per cent | Total | Per cent |
|---|---|---|---|---|---|---|---|---|
| 0-9 | 71 | 22.7 | 634 | 22.0 | 1,099 | 22.0 | 926 | 21.3 |

TABLE A-1 *(continued)*

|  | 1891 | | 1911 | | 1931 | | 1951 | |
|---|---|---|---|---|---|---|---|---|
|  | Total | Per cent | Total | Per cent | Total | Per cent | Total | Per cent |
| 10-14 | 27 | 8.6 | 215 | 7.5 | 556 | 11.1 | 376 | 8.6 |
| 15-24 | 68 | 21.8 | 608 | 21.1 | 957 | 19.1 | 659 | 15.2 |
| 25-64 | 143 | 45.6 | 1,368 | 47.6 | 2,210 | 44.2 | 1,991 | 45.8 |
| 65+ | 4 | 1.4 | 50 | 1.8 | 179 | 3.6 | 393 | 9.0 |
| 10+ | 242 | 77.3 | 2,241 | 78.0 | 3,902 | 78.0 | 3,419 | 78.7 |
| All ages | 313 | 100.0 | 2,875 | 100.0 | 5,001 | 100.0 | 4,345 | 100.0 |
| **FEMALE** | | | | | | | | |
| 0-9 | 68 | 31.6 | 614 | 30.8 | 1,066 | 25.3 | 889 | 22.3 |
| 10-14 | 25 | 11.5 | 207 | 10.4 | 544 | 12.9 | 361 | 9.1 |
| 15-24 | 42 | 19.6 | 377 | 18.9 | 873 | 20.7 | 651 | 16.5 |
| 25-64 | 78 | 35.9 | 763 | 38.2 | 1,602 | 37.9 | 1,790 | 45.1 |
| 65+ | 3 | 1.5 | 35 | 1.7 | 133 | 3.1 | 279 | 7.0 |
| 10+ | 148 | 68.4 | 1,382 | 69.2 | 3,152 | 74.7 | 3,081 | 77.7 |
| All ages | 216 | 100.0 | 1,996 | 100.0 | 4,218 | 100.0 | 3,970 | 100.0 |

*Alberta*

MALE

| | | | | | | | | |
|---|---|---|---|---|---|---|---|---|
| 0-9 | (a) | (a) | 448 | 20.4 | 803 | 20.1 | 1,069 | 21.8 |
| 10-14 | ,, | ,, | 166 | 7.6 | 405 | 10.1 | 390 | 7.9 |
| 15-24 | ,, | ,, | 451 | 20.8 | 724 | 18.1 | 762 | 15.5 |
| 25-64 | ,, | ,, | 1,096 | 50.0 | 1,921 | 48.1 | 2,314 | 47.1 |
| 65+ | ,, | ,, | 36 | 1.6 | 149 | 3.8 | 387 | 7.9 |
| 10+ | ,, | ,, | 1,749 | 79.6 | 3,199 | 79.9 | 3,853 | 78.2 |
| All ages | ,, | ,, | 2,197 | 100.0 | 4,002 | 100.0 | 4,922 | 100.0 |
| **FEMALE** | | | | | | | | |
| 0-9 | (a) | (a) | 431 | 28.8 | 791 | 23.9 | 1,029 | 23.0 |
| 10-14 | ,, | ,, | 157 | 10.5 | 390 | 11.7 | 379 | 8.5 |
| 15-24 | ,, | ,, | 281 | 18.8 | 669 | 20.2 | 683 | 16.4 |
| 25-64 | ,, | ,, | 601 | 40.2 | 1,356 | 40.9 | 2,049 | 45.8 |
| 65+ | ,, | ,, | 25 | 1.6 | 108 | 3.3 | 282 | 6.4 |
| 10+ | ,, | ,, | 1,064 | 71.2 | 2,523 | 76.1 | 3,393 | 77.0 |
| All ages | ,, | ,, | 1,495 | 100.0 | 3,314 | 100.0 | 4,423 | 100.0 |

*British Columbia*

MALE

| | | | | | | | | |
|---|---|---|---|---|---|---|---|---|
| 0-9 | 91 | 14.7 | 330 | 13.3 | 563 | 14.6 | 1,152 | 19.3 |
| 10-14 | 37 | 5.9 | 130 | 5.2 | 302 | 7.9 | 398 | 6.7 |
| 15-24 | 115 | 18.4 | 460 | 18.4 | 609 | 15.9 | 752 | 12.6 |
| 25-64 | 364 | 58.8 | 1,518 | 60.9 | 2,146 | 56.0 | 2,969 | 49.7 |
| 65+ | 15 | 2.3 | 53 | 2.2 | 234 | 5.8 | 700 | 11.7 |
| 10+ | 531 | 85.3 | 2,161 | 86.7 | 3,291 | 85.4 | 4,819 | 80.7 |
| All ages | 622 | 100.0 | 2,491 | 100.0 | 3,854 | 100.0 | 5,971 | 100.0 |
| **FEMALE** | | | | | | | | |
| 0-9 | 89 | 25.8 | 323 | 23.2 | 549 | 17.8 | 1,106 | 19.5 |

TABLE A-1 (continued)

|  | 1891 | | 1911 | | 1931 | | 1951 | |
|---|---|---|---|---|---|---|---|---|
|  | Total | Per cent | Total | Per cent | Total | Per cent | Total | Per cent |
| 10-14 | 34 | 9.8 | 124 | 8.9 | 296 | 9.6 | 388 | 6.8 |
| 15-24 | 68 | 19.7 | 255 | 18.2 | 572 | 18.6 | 749 | 13.2 |
| 25-64 | 146 | 42.2 | 660 | 47.3 | 1,511 | 49.0 | 2,878 | 50.7 |
| 65+ | 9 | 2.5 | 34 | 2.4 | 161 | 5.1 | 562 | 9.8 |
| 10+ | 257 | 74.2 | 1,073 | 76.8 | 2,540 | 82.2 | 4,577 | 80.5 |
| All ages | 346 | 100.0 | 1,396 | 100.0 | 3,089 | 100.0 | 5,683 | 100.0 |

*Canada*

MALE

| 0-9 | 6,031 | 23.7 | 8,418 | 21.7 | 11,141 | 20.6 | 15,361 | 22.6 |
|---|---|---|---|---|---|---|---|---|
| 10-14 | 2,800 | 10.6 | 3,547 | 9.2 | 5,423 | 10.3 | 5,557 | 8.4 |
| 15-24 | 4,956 | 20.5 | 7,361 | 19.7 | 9,878 | 18.5 | 10,383 | 14.8 |
| 25-64 | 9,349 | 41.4 | 16,846 | 45.2 | 24,260 | 44.8 | 32,184 | 45.6 |
| 65+ | 1,145 | 4.0 | 1,684 | 4.4 | 2,868 | 5.9 | 5,387 | 8.6 |
| 10+ | 18,250 | 76.3 | 29,438 | 78.3 | 42,429 | 79.5 | 53,511 | 77.4 |
| All ages | 24,281 | 100.0 | 37,856 | 100.0 | 53,570 | 100.0 | 68,872 | 100.0 |

FEMALE

| 0-9 | 5,860 | 26.6 | 8,263 | 25.3 | 10,897 | 22.1 | 14,719 | 22.5 |
|---|---|---|---|---|---|---|---|---|
| 10-14 | 2,694 | 11.4 | 3,451 | 10.3 | 5,304 | 11.1 | 5,369 | 8.4 |
| 15-24 | 4,902 | 20.4 | 6,488 | 19.3 | 9,608 | 19.3 | 10,416 | 15.5 |
| 25-64 | 8,911 | 37.8 | 13,861 | 40.6 | 21,328 | 41.7 | 31,548 | 45.6 |
| 65+ | 1,041 | 3.8 | 1,642 | 4.5 | 2,834 | 5.8 | 5,231 | 8.1 |
| 10+ | 17,548 | 73.4 | 25,443 | 74.7 | 39,074 | 77.9 | 52,564 | 77.5 |
| All ages | 23,408 | 100.0 | 33,705 | 100.0 | 49,971 | 100.0 | 67,283 | 100.0 |

MALE AND FEMALE

| 0-9 | 11,891 | 24.9 | 16,681 | 23.3 | 22,038 | 21.3 | 30,080 | 22.1 |
|---|---|---|---|---|---|---|---|---|
| 10-14 | 5,494 | 11.5 | 6,998 | 9.8 | 10,727 | 10.4 | 10,926 | 8.0 |
| 15-24 | 9,858 | 20.7 | 13,849 | 19.4 | 19,486 | 18.8 | 20,799 | 15.3 |
| 25-64 | 18,260 | 38.3 | 30,707 | 42.9 | 45,588 | 44.0 | 63,732 | 46.8 |
| 65+ | 2,186 | 4.6 | 3,326 | 4.6 | 5,702 | 5.5 | 10,618 | 7.8 |
| 10+ | 35,798 | 75.1 | 54,881 | 76.7 | 81,503 | 78.7 | 106,075 | 77.9 |
| All ages | 47,689 | 100.0 | 71,561 | 100.0 | 103,541 | 100.0 | 136,155 | 100.0 |

NOTE: (a) In this and the following tables, data for Yukon, Northwest Territories, and Alberta are included with Saskatchewan for 1891.

SOURCE: 1891, 1911, 1931 – *Census of Canada, 1931*, vol I, 388-93; 1951 – *Census of Canada, 1951*, vol I, Table 21.

TABLE A-2

Gainfully occupied, 1911 and 1931, and labour force 1951, distribution, total, and percentage (00 omitted)

| | 1891 | | 1911 | | 1931 | | 1951 | |
|---|---|---|---|---|---|---|---|---|
| | Total | Per cent | Total | Per cent | Total | Per cent | Total | Per cent |

*Prince Edward Island*

MALE

| | | | | | | | | |
|---|---|---|---|---|---|---|---|---|
| 10-14 | — | — | 1 | 0.4 | 2 | 0.7 | — | — |
| 15-25 | — | — | 75 | 26.8 | 68 | 24.5 | 58 | 20.6 |
| 25-64 | — | — | 176 | 62.9 | 176 | 63.3 | 199 | 70.8 |
| 65+ | — | — | 28 | 10.0 | 32 | 11.5 | 24 | 8.5 |
| Total | 313 | 100.0 | 280 | 100.0 | 278 | 100.0 | 281 | 100.0 |

FEMALE

| | | | | | | | | |
|---|---|---|---|---|---|---|---|---|
| 10-14 | — | — | — | — | — | — | — | — |
| 15-24 | — | — | 18 | 45.0 | 20 | 46.5 | 26 | 43.3 |
| 25-64 | — | — | 19 | 47.5 | 20 | 46.5 | 31 | 51.7 |
| 65+ | — | — | 3 | 7.5 | 3 | 7.0 | 3 | 5.0 |
| Total | 40 | 100.0 | 40 | 100.0 | 43 | 100.0 | 60 | 100.0 |

*Nova Scotia*

MALE

| | | | | | | | | |
|---|---|---|---|---|---|---|---|---|
| 10-14 | — | — | 11 | 0.7 | 5 | 0.3 | 2 | 0.1 |
| 15-24 | — | — | 376 | 25.3 | 354 | 23.1 | 342 | 19.2 |
| 25-64 | — | — | 977 | 65.6 | 1,037 | 67.7 | 1,328 | 74.6 |
| 65+ | — | — | 125 | 8.4 | 135 | 8.8 | 109 | 6.1 |
| Total | 1,349 | 100.0 | 1,489 | 100.0 | 1,531 | 100.0 | 1,781 | 100.0 |

FEMALE

| | | | | | | | | |
|---|---|---|---|---|---|---|---|---|
| 10-14 | — | — | 4 | 1.6 | 1 | 0.4 | — | — |
| 15-24 | — | — | 120 | 49.0 | 132 | 47.5 | 170 | 39.8 |
| 25-64 | — | — | 110 | 44.9 | 132 | 47.5 | 243 | 56.9 |
| 65+ | — | — | 11 | 4.5 | 13 | 4.7 | 14 | 3.3 |
| Total | 225 | 100.0 | 245 | 100.0 | 278 | 100.0 | 427 | 100.0 |

*New Brunswick*

MALE

| | | | | | | | | |
|---|---|---|---|---|---|---|---|---|
| 10-14 | — | — | 6 | 0.6 | 9 | 0.8 | 2 | 0.1 |
| 15-24 | — | — | 269 | 26.0 | 296 | 25.1 | 270 | 20.0 |
| 25-65 | — | — | 684 | 66.2 | 788 | 66.8 | 1,003 | 74.3 |
| 65+ | — | — | 74 | 7.2 | 87 | 7.4 | 75 | 5.6 |
| Total | 941 | 100.0 | 1,033 | 100.0 | 1,180 | 100.0 | 1,350 | 100.0 |

FEMALE

| | | | | | | | | |
|---|---|---|---|---|---|---|---|---|
| 10-14 | — | — | 3 | 1.8 | 1 | 0.5 | 1 | 0.3 |
| 15-24 | — | — | 81 | 48.8 | 109 | 49.5 | 147 | 43.1 |
| 25-64 | — | — | 76 | 45.8 | 102 | 46.4 | 184 | 54.0 |
| 65+ | — | — | 6 | 3.6 | 8 | 3.6 | 9 | 2.6 |
| Total | 134 | 100.0 | 166 | 100.0 | 220 | 100.0 | 341 | 100.0 |

TABLE A-2 (continued)

|  | 1891 | | 1911 | | 1931 | | 1951 | |
|---|---|---|---|---|---|---|---|---|
|  | Total | Per cent | Total | Per cent | Total | Per cent | Total | Per cent |

*Quebec*

MALE

| 10-14 | — | — | 56 | 1.0 | 100 | 1.2 | 35 | 0.3 |
| 15-24 | — | — | 1,594 | 28.9 | 2,169 | 26.3 | 2,536 | 22.4 |
| 25-64 | — | — | 3,631 | 65.8 | 5,623 | 68.3 | 8,318 | 73.6 |
| 65+ | — | — | 240 | 4.3 | 341 | 4.1 | 413 | 3.7 |
| Total | 3,988 | 100.0 | 5,521 | 100.0 | 8,233 | 100.0 | 11,302 | 100.0 |

FEMALE

| 10-14 | — | — | 27 | 2.7 | 16 | 0.8 | 11 | 0.3 |
| 15-24 | — | — | 502 | 49.6 | 1,004 | 49.6 | 1,489 | 43.6 |
| 25-64 | — | — | 455 | 45.0 | 954 | 47.1 | 1,848 | 54.1 |
| 65+ | — | — | 28 | 2.8 | 50 | 2.5 | 69 | 2.0 |
| Total | 531 | 100.0 | 1,012 | 100.0 | 2,024 | 100.0 | 3,417 | 100.0 |

*Ontario*

MALE

| 10-14 | — | — | 69 | 0.8 | 27 | 0.2 | 19 | 0.1 |
| 15-24 | — | — | 2,119 | 25.3 | 2,267 | 20.7 | 2,566 | 17.8 |
| 25-64 | — | — | 5,758 | 68.9 | 8,049 | 73.4 | 10,994 | 76.4 |
| 65+ | — | — | 415 | 5.0 | 622 | 5.7 | 820 | 5.7 |
| Total | 6,358 | 100.0 | 8,361 | 100.0 | 10,965 | 100.0 | 14,399 | 100.0 |

FEMALE

| 10-14 | — | — | 32 | 2.1 | 4 | 0.2 | 6 | 0.1 |
| 15-24 | — | — | 767 | 49.5 | 1,128 | 45.2 | 1,555 | 34.9 |
| 25-64 | — | — | 715 | 46.2 | 1,296 | 51.9 | 2,772 | 62.3 |
| 65+ | — | — | 35 | 2.3 | 67 | 2.7 | 118 | 2.7 |
| Total | 948 | 100.0 | 1,549 | 100.0 | 2,495 | 100.0 | 4,451 | 100.0 |

*Manitoba*

MALE

| 10-14 | — | — | 10 | 0.6 | 9 | 0.4 | 4 | 0.2 |
| 15-24 | — | — | 426 | 27.3 | 523 | 23.2 | 429 | 18.5 |
| 25-64 | — | — | 1,090 | 69.9 | 1,631 | 72.2 | 1,765 | 76.0 |
| 65+ | — | — | 34 | 2.2 | 96 | 4.2 | 124 | 5.3 |
| Total | 506 | 100.0 | 1,560 | 100.0 | 2,259 | 100.0 | 2,322 | 100.0 |

FEMALE

| 10-14 | — | — | 5 | 2.2 | 1 | 0.2 | 1 | 0.2 |
| 15-24 | — | — | 120 | 53.8 | 234 | 52.1 | 252 | 38.1 |
| 25-64 | — | — | 96 | 43.0 | 206 | 45.9 | 396 | 59.8 |
| 65+ | — | — | 2 | 0.9 | 8 | 1.8 | 13 | 2.0 |
| Total | 44 | 100.0 | 223 | 100.0 | 449 | 100.0 | 662 | 100.0 |

TABLE A-2 *(continued)*

| | 1891 | | 1911 | | 1931 | | 1951 | |
|---|---|---|---|---|---|---|---|---|
| | Total | Per cent | Total | Per cent | Total | Per cent | Total | Per cent |

*Saskatchewan*

MALE
| | | | | | | | | |
|---|---|---|---|---|---|---|---|---|
| 10-14 | — | — | 6 | 0.3 | 7 | 0.2 | 4 | 0.2 |
| 15-24 | — | — | 552 | 28.3 | 747 | 24.8 | 478 | 19.0 |
| 25-64 | — | — | 1,359 | 69.6 | 2,155 | 71.5 | 1,869 | 74.4 |
| 65+ | — | — | 35 | 1.8 | 105 | 3.5 | 161 | 6.4 |
| Total | 208 | 100.0 | 1,952 | 100.0 | 3,014 | 100.0 | 2,512 | 100.0 |

FEMALE
| | | | | | | | | |
|---|---|---|---|---|---|---|---|---|
| 10-14 | — | — | 3 | 2.3 | 1 | 0.3 | 1 | 0.2 |
| 15-24 | — | — | 66 | 50.0 | 200 | 53.2 | 217 | 42.5 |
| 25-64 | — | — | 62 | 46.2 | 166 | 44.1 | 282 | 55.3 |
| 65+ | — | — | 2 | 1.5 | 9 | 2.4 | 10 | 2.0 |
| Total | 10 | 100.0 | 132 | 100.0 | 376 | 100.0 | 510 | 100.0 |

*Alberta*

MALE
| | | | | | | | | |
|---|---|---|---|---|---|---|---|---|
| 10-14 | (a) | (a) | 5 | 0.3 | 4 | 0.2 | 3 | 0.1 |
| 15-24 | ,, | ,, | 393 | 26.3 | 548 | 21.7 | 565 | 19.4 |
| 25-64 | ,, | ,, | 1,074 | 71.7 | 1,879 | 74.3 | 2,193 | 75.3 |
| 65+ | ,, | ,, | 25 | 1.7 | 97 | 3.8 | 152 | 5.2 |
| Total | ,, | ,, | 1,497 | 100.0 | 2,528 | 100.0 | 2,913 | 100.0 |

FEMALE
| | | | | | | | | |
|---|---|---|---|---|---|---|---|---|
| 10-14 | (a) | (a) | 3 | 2.5 | — | — | 1 | 0.2 |
| 15-24 | ,, | ,, | 57 | 47.5 | 169 | 50.4 | 259 | 41.3 |
| 25-64 | ,, | ,, | 58 | 48.3 | 159 | 47.5 | 355 | 56.6 |
| 65+ | ,, | ,, | 2 | 1.7 | 7 | 2.1 | 12 | 1.9 |
| Total | ,, | ,, | 120 | 100.0 | 335 | 100.0 | 627 | 100.0 |

*British Columbia*

MALE
| | | | | | | | | |
|---|---|---|---|---|---|---|---|---|
| 10-14 | — | — | 8 | 0.4 | 3 | 0.1 | 4 | 0.1 |
| 15-24 | — | — | 406 | 21.4 | 433 | 16.5 | 536 | 15.5 |
| 25-64 | — | — | 1,450 | 76.6 | 2,065 | 78.7 | 2,716 | 78.4 |
| 65+ | — | — | 30 | 1.6 | 124 | 4.7 | 207 | 6.0 |
| Total | 445 | 100.0 | 1,894 | 100.0 | 2,625 | 100.0 | 3,463 | 100.0 |

FEMALE
| | | | | | | | | |
|---|---|---|---|---|---|---|---|---|
| 10-14 | — | — | 2 | 1.2 | 1 | 0.2 | 1 | 0.1 |
| 15-24 | — | — | 70 | 42.2 | 208 | 47.5 | 317 | 32.3 |
| 25-64 | — | — | 92 | 55.4 | 221 | 50.5 | 641 | 65.4 |
| 65+ | — | — | 2 | 1.2 | 8 | 1.8 | 21 | 2.1 |
| Total | 31 | 100.0 | 166 | 100.0 | 438 | 100.0 | 980 | 100.0 |

TABLE A-2 *(continued)*

|  | 1891 | | 1911 | | 1931 | | 1951 | |
|---|---|---|---|---|---|---|---|---|
|  | Total | Per cent | Total | Per cent | Total | Per cent | Total | Per cent |
| *Canada* | | | | | | | | |
| MALE | | | | | | | | |
| 10-14 | — | — | 172 | 0.7 | 166 | 0.5 | 73 | 0.2 |
| 15-24 | — | — | 6,210 | 26.3 | 7,407 | 22.7 | 7,780 | 19.3 |
| 25-64 | — | — | 16,199 | 68.7 | 23,403 | 71.8 | 30,385 | 75.4 |
| 65+ | — | — | 1,006 | 4.3 | 1,638 | 5.0 | 2,085 | 5.2 |
| Total | 14,108 | 100.0 | 23,587 | 100.0 | 32,614 | 100.0 | 40,323 | 100.0 |
| FEMALE | | | | | | | | |
| 10-14 | — | — | 79 | 2.2 | 25 | 0.4 | 22 | 0.2 |
| 15-24 | — | — | 1,801 | 49.3 | 3,204 | 48.1 | 4,432 | 38.6 |
| 25-64 | — | — | 1,682 | 46.0 | 3,255 | 48.9 | 6,752 | 58.8 |
| 65+ | — | — | 91 | 2.5 | 174 | 2.6 | 269 | 2.3 |
| Total | 1,963 | 100.0 | 3,653 | 100.0 | 6,659 | 100.0 | 11,475 | 100.0 |

SOURCE:   1891 – *Census of Canada, 1891*, vol II, Table XII; 1911 – *Census of Canada, 1911*, vol VI, Table 5; 1931 – *Census of Canada, 1931*, vol VII, Table 56; 1951 – *Census of Canada, 1951*, vol IV, Table 19.

TABLE A-3

Age-sex specific participation rates for the gainfully occupied, 1891, 1911, and 1931 and for the labour force, 1951

|  | 1891 | 1911 | 1931 | 1951 |
|---|---|---|---|---|
| *Prince Edward Island* | | | | |
| MALE | | | | |
| 10+ | 76.3 | 76.1 | 77.4 | 73.6 |
| 10-14 | — | 1.8 | 4.2 | — |
| 15-24 | — | 80.6 | 80.0 | 77.3 |
| 25-64 | — | 96.7 | 96.7 | 94.3 |
| 65+ | — | 73.7 | 72.7 | 50.0 |
| Total male | 57.0 | 59.6 | 61.2 | 56.0 |
| FEMALE | | | | |
| 10+ | 9.8 | 10.9 | 12.9 | 16.4 |
| 10-14 | — | — | — | — |
| 15-24 | — | 19.4 | 26.7 | 35.6 |
| 25-64 | — | 10.3 | 11.7 | 15.6 |
| 65+ | — | 7.3 | 7.0 | 6.1 |
| Total female | 7.4 | 8.5 | 10.1 | 12.4 |
| Total M+F – 10+ | 43.1 | 43.5 | 46.3 | 45.6 |
| Total M+F | 32.4 | 34.1 | 36.4 | 34.7 |

TABLE A-3 *(continued)*

|  | 1891 | 1911 | 1931 | 1951 |
|---|---|---|---|---|
| *Nova Scotia* | | | | |
| MALE | | | | |
| 10+ | 78.2 | 77.4 | 73.9 | 71.9 |
| 10-14 | — | 4.2 | 1.7 | 0.7 |
| 15-24 | — | 79.2 | 70.5 | 70.1 |
| 25-64 | — | 96.5 | 96.0 | 93.4 |
| 65+ | — | 71.4 | 67.2 | 40.1 |
| Total male | 59.5 | 59.5 | 58.2 | 54.8 |
| FEMALE | | | | |
| 10+ | 13.2 | 13.3 | 14.2 | 17.5 |
| 10-14 | — | 1.6 | 0.4 | — |
| 15-24 | — | 26.0 | 28.5 | 34.7 |
| 25-64 | — | 11.6 | 13.1 | 17.6 |
| 65+ | — | 5.9 | 6.3 | 5.1 |
| Total female | 10.1 | 10.2 | 11.1 | 13.4 |
| Total M+F – 10+ | 45.8 | 46.0 | 45.0 | 44.9 |
| Total M+F | 35.0 | 35.3 | 35.3 | 34.4 |
| *New Brunswick* | | | | |
| MALE | | | | |
| 10+ | 77.1 | 76.1 | 74.2 | 70.8 |
| 10-14 | — | 3.1 | 3.8 | .8 |
| 15-24 | — | 78.7 | 74.7 | 70.5 |
| 25-64 | — | 96.5 | 96.3 | 93.1 |
| 65+ | — | 67.3 | 62.1 | 38.3 |
| Total male | 57.5 | 57.6 | 56.5 | 52.1 |
| FEMALE | | | | |
| 10+ | 11.4 | 12.8 | 14.6 | 17.9 |
| 10-14 | — | 1.6 | 0.4 | 0.4 |
| 15-24 | — | 24.3 | 28.9 | 35.8 |
| 25-64 | — | 11.4 | 13.2 | 17.4 |
| 65+ | — | 5.7 | 6.0 | 4.6 |
| Total female | 8.5 | 9.7 | 11.0 | 13.3 |
| Total M+F – 10+ | 44.8 | 45.3 | 45.1 | 44.3 |
| Total M+F | 33.5 | 34.1 | 34.3 | 32.8 |
| *Quebec* | | | | |
| MALE | | | | |
| 10+ | 74.8 | 75.3 | 75.4 | 74.9 |
| **10-14** | — | 5.0 | 6.3 | 1.9 |
| 15-24 | — | 83.2 | 77.9 | 76.3 |
| 25-64 | — | 94.5 | 95.9 | 94.5 |
| 65+ | — | 52.6 | 49.8 | 36.4 |
| Total male | 53.7 | 54.8 | 56.9 | 55.9 |

TABLE A-3 *(continued)*

|  | 1891 | 1911 | 1931 | 1951 |
|---|---|---|---|---|
| **FEMALE** | | | | |
| 10+ | 9.9 | 14.1 | 18.8 | 22.2 |
| 10-14 | — | 2.4 | 1.0 | 0.6 |
| 15-24 | — | 26.3 | 34.8 | 43.0 |
| 25-64 | — | 12.3 | 17.0 | 20.6 |
| 65+ | — | 6.1 | 7.2 | 5.8 |
| Total female | 7.1 | 10.2 | 14.2 | 16.8 |
| | | | | |
| Total M+F – 10+ | 42.2 | 45.0 | 47.3 | 48.2 |
| Total M+F | 30.4 | 32.7 | 35.7 | 36.3 |

*Ontario*

|  | 1891 | 1911 | 1931 | 1951 |
|---|---|---|---|---|
| **MALE** | | | | |
| 10+ | 77.6 | 80.4 | 77.5 | 78.0 |
| 10-14 | — | 5.8 | 1.7 | 1.1 |
| 15-24 | — | 84.5 | 72.9 | 76.1 |
| 25-64 | — | 96.2 | 96.3 | 95.4 |
| 65+ | — | 58.0 | 54.1 | 43.1 |
| Total male | 59.6 | 64.5 | 62.7 | 62.2 |
| | | | | |
| **FEMALE** | | | | |
| 10+ | 11.8 | 15.9 | 18.2 | 24.2 |
| 10-14 | — | 2.8 | 0.3 | 0.4 |
| 15-24 | — | 32.6 | 37.7 | 47.0 |
| 25-64 | — | 12.9 | 16.4 | 24.4 |
| 65+ | — | 5.0 | 5.6 | 5.6 |
| Total female | 9.1 | 12.7 | 14.8 | 19.5 |
| | | | | |
| Total M+F – 10+ | 45.0 | 49.2 | 48.4 | 51.2 |
| Total M+F | 34.7 | 39.3 | 39.2 | 41.0 |

*Manitoba*

|  | 1891 | 1911 | 1931 | 1951 |
|---|---|---|---|---|
| **MALE** | | | | |
| 10+ | 84.2 | 81.3 | 76.3 | 74.5 |
| 10-14 | — | 4.5 | 2.3 | 1.3 |
| 15-24 | — | 83.9 | 73.4 | 75.2 |
| 25-64 | — | 96.4 | 96.9 | 93.6 |
| 65+ | — | 56.7 | 55.5 | 35.0 |
| Total male | 62.0 | 62.4 | 61.4 | 58.8 |
| | | | | |
| **FEMALE** | | | | |
| 10+ | 9.8 | 14.8 | 17.2 | 21.9 |
| 10-14 | — | 2.3 | 0.3 | 0.3 |
| 15-24 | — | 28.3 | 33.4 | 42.8 |
| 25-64 | — | 11.8 | 14.7 | 21.5 |
| 65+ | — | 4.0 | 5.6 | 4.3 |
| Total female | 6.7 | 10.8 | 13.5 | 17.3 |

TABLE A-3 (continued)

|  | 1891 | 1911 | 1931 | 1951 |
|---|---|---|---|---|
| Total M+F – 10+ | 52.5 | 52.1 | 48.5 | 48.6 |
| Total M+F | 37.4 | 39.0 | 38.7 | 38.4 |

*Saskatchewan*

MALE
| 10+ | 86.0 | 87.1 | 77.2 | 73.5 |
|---|---|---|---|---|
| 10-14 | — | 2.8 | 1.3 | 1.1 |
| 15-24 | — | 90.8 | 78.1 | 72.5 |
| 25-64 | — | 99.3 | 97.5 | 93.9 |
| 65+ | — | 70.0 | 59.3 | 41.0 |
| Total male | 66.5 | 67.9 | 60.3 | 57.8 |

FEMALE
| 10+ | 6.7 | 9.6 | 11.9 | 16.5 |
|---|---|---|---|---|
| 10-14 | — | 1.4 | 0.2 | 0.3 |
| 15-24 | — | 17.5 | 22.9 | 33.3 |
| 25-64 | — | 8.0 | 10.4 | 15.8 |
| 65+ | — | 5.7 | 6.8 | 3.6 |
| Total female | 4.6 | 6.6 | 8.9 | 12.8 |

| Total M+F – 10+ | 55.8 | 57.5 | 48.1 | 46.5 |
|---|---|---|---|---|
| Total M+F | 41.1 | 42.8 | 36.8 | 36.3 |

*Alberta*

MALE
| 10+ | (a) | 85.6 | 78.0 | 75.6 |
|---|---|---|---|---|
| 10-14 | ,, | 3.0 | 1.0 | 0.8 |
| 15-24 | ,, | 86.9 | 75.7 | 74.1 |
| 25-64 | ,, | 98.1 | 97.8 | 94.8 |
| 65+ | ,, | 69.4 | 65.1 | 39.3 |
| Total male | ,, | 68.1 | 63.2 | 59.2 |

FEMALE
| 10+ | (a) | 11.3 | 13.3 | 18.2 |
|---|---|---|---|---|
| 10-14 | ,, | 1.9 | — | 0.3 |
| 15-24 | ,, | 20.3 | 25.3 | 37.9 |
| 25-64 | ,, | 9.6 | 11.7 | 17.3 |
| 65+ | ,, | 8.0 | 6.5 | 4.3 |
| Total female | ,, | 8.0 | 10.1 | 14.0 |

| Total M+F – 10+ | (a) | 57.5 | 50.0 | 48.5 |
|---|---|---|---|---|
| Total M+F | ,, | 43.8 | 39.1 | 37.7 |

*British Columbia*

MALE
| 10+ | 83.8 | 87.7 | 80.1 | 71.9 |
|---|---|---|---|---|
| 10-14 | — | 6.2 | 1.0 | 1.0 |

TABLE A-3 (continued)

|  | 1891 | 1911 | 1931 | 1951 |
|---|---|---|---|---|
| 15-24 | — | 88.3 | 71.1 | 71.3 |
| 25-64 | — | 95.6 | 96.3 | 91.5 |
| 65+ | — | 57.7 | 56.1 | 29.6 |
| Total male | 71.7 | 76.1 | 68.4 | 58.0 |
| FEMALE |  |  |  |  |
| 10+ | 12.1 | 15.5 | 17.2 | 21.4 |
| 10-14 | — | 1.6 | 0.3 | 0.3 |
| 15-24 | — | 27.5 | 36.3 | 42.3 |
| 25-64 | — | 13.9 | 14.6 | 22.3 |
| 65+ | — | 5.9 | 5.0 | 3.7 |
| Total female | 9.0 | 11.9 | 14.2 | 17.2 |
| Total M+F – 10+ | 60.4 | 63.8 | 52.7 | 47.3 |
| Total M+F | 49.2 | 53.0 | 44.2 | 38.1 |

Canada

| MALE |  |  |  |  |
|---|---|---|---|---|
| 10+ | 77.3 | 80.1 | 76.9 | 75.3 |
| 10-14 | — | 4.8 | 3.1 | 1.3 |
| 15-24 | — | 84.4 | 75.0 | 74.9 |
| 25-64 | — | 96.2 | 96.5 | 94.4 |
| 65+ | — | 59.4 | 55.7 | 38.7 |
| Total male | 58.1 | 62.3 | 60.8 | 58.5 |
| FEMALE |  |  |  |  |
| 10+ | 11.2 | 14.4 | 17.0 | 21.8 |
| 10-14 | — | 2.3 | 0.5 | 0.4 |
| 15-24 | — | 27.8 | 33.3 | 42.3 |
| 25-64 | — | 12.1 | 15.3 | 21.4 |
| 65+ | — | 5.5 | 6.2 | 5.1 |
| Total female | 8.4 | 10.8 | 13.3 | 17.0 |
| Total M+F – 10+ | 44.9 | 49.6 | 48.2 | 48.8 |
| Total M+F | 33.7 | 38.1 | 37.9 | 38.0 |

SOURCES AND METHOD: For sources see Tables A-1 and A-2. The participation rates were derived by dividing the labour force data of Table A-2 by the respective age and sex data of Table A-1.

# APPENDIX B
# Gross Value Added Estimates

To DETERMINE provincial output levels census value added was estimated for each of the major industrial components.[1] Value added, when the maximum amount of data exists, is computed by deducting from the total value of shipments (exclusive of excise and manufacturers' sales taxes and adjusted for changes in inventory of finished goods and goods-in-process for each industry) the cost of materials, fuel, purchased electricity, and process supplies consumed in the production process (depreciation, of course, is still part of the residual). These value added residuals, however, are not exactly equivalent to gross domestic product originating in these industries, because they still contain miscellaneous indirect taxes such as licenses and property taxes as well as the cost of services such as insurance, advertising, communications, etc., which originate in the non-commodity–producing industries.

Even at the present time the data necessary to make these "service" deductions have not been collected by the Dominion Bureau of Statistics. These charges, however, appear to play a less important role in the agriculture and mining industries than in manufacturing and construction. Thus the GDP estimates for the former industries, in provinces largely dominated by their production, will be proportionately greater than the value added data.

This method of computation applies only to the commodity-producing group of industries. Here, for the purpose of the GVA estimates, the value added in the service sector was calculated separately by the method described below. The estimates for 1929 and 1956 of the commodity industries by provinces were collected in the manner described above. The sectors included were agriculture, fishing and trapping, forestry (for 1956 but not for 1929), mining, manufacturing, construction (for 1956 but not for 1929), and utilities (electric power). These estimates appear in the *Survey of Production, 1961*, a publication of the Dominion Bureau of Statistics.

The value added estimates of the commodity and non-commodity-producing sectors for 1890 and 1910 were derived by the method outlined by Firestone in *Canada's Economic Development, 1867-1953*.[2] The approach used to collect the data in Tables B 1-4, was first to re-estimate Firestone's countrywide totals as closely as possible following his methodology. Then, since the data for the earlier years came from the decennial censuses, this method was repeated using

TABLE B-1

Gross value added (current dollars), by sectors, for provinces, 1890 ($ millions)

| Provinces | Agriculture (1) | Fishing and trapping (2) | Forestry (3) | Mining (4) | Manufacturing (5) | Construction (6) | Transportation (7) | Personal and professional services (8) | Domestic trade (9) | Government (10) | Total 1-10 (11) |
|---|---|---|---|---|---|---|---|---|---|---|---|
| 1. P.E.I. | 6.3 | 0.8 | 0.6 | — | 2.0 | 0.3 | 0.1 | 2.4 | 1.3 | 0.3 | 14.1 |
| 2. Nova Scotia | 11.6 | 4.5 | 3.6 | 3.9 | 13.3 | 2.6 | 2.3 | 12.7 | 7.4 | 2.2 | 64.1 |
| 3. New Brunswick | 10.0 | 2.3 | 5.8 | 0.1 | 9.8 | 4.8 | 1.4 | 7.7 | 5.7 | 1.5 | 49.1 |
| 4. Quebec | 47.7 | 1.5 | 15.7 | 1.3 | 57.7 | 7.8 | 5.0 | 30.9 | 31.5 | 9.6 | 208.7 |
| 5. Ontario | 117.5 | 1.4 | 26.2 | 1.7 | 96.1 | 21.1 | 8.1 | 55.3 | 49.6 | 14.2 | 391.2 |
| 6. Manitoba | 16.8 | 0.2 | 0.9 | — | 3.8 | 0.2 | 0.6 | 3.0 | 3.7 | 1.1 | 30.3 |
| 7. Saskatchewan | 4.1 | 0.1 | 0.5 | — | 0.9 | 0.5 | 0.3 | 1.2 | 0.9 | 1.2 | 9.7 |
| 8. Alberta | (a) | (a) | (a) | (a) | (a) | (a) | (a) | (a) | (a) | (a) | (a) |
| 9. British Columbia | 3.2 | 2.2 | 1.4 | 2.4 | 6.1 | 1.3 | 0.8 | 3.7 | 3.2 | 1.8 | 26.1 |
| 10. Canada | 217.2 | 13.0 | 54.7 | 9.4 | 189.7 | 38.6 | 18.6 | 116.9 | 103.3 | 31.9 | 793.3 |

NOTE: (a) Alberta and the Northwest Territories were included with the Saskatchewan returns.

TABLE B-2

Gross value added (current dollars), by sectors, for provinces, 1910 ($ millions)

| Provinces | Agriculture (1) | Fishing and trapping (2) | Forestry (3) | Mining (4) | Manufacturing (5) | Construction (6) | Transportation (7) | Personal and professional services (8) | Domestic trade (9) | Government (10) | Total 1-10 (11) |
|---|---|---|---|---|---|---|---|---|---|---|---|
| 1. P.E.I. | 8.2 | 0.8 | 0.5 | — | 1.2 | 0.2 | 1.1 | 2.1 | 1.7 | 0.2 | 16.0 |
| 2. Nova Scotia | 17.0 | 6.5 | 6.9 | 14.9 | 23.0 | 5.5 | 10.7 | 13.6 | 12.3 | 3.8 | 114.2 |
| 3. New Brunswick | 14.5 | 2.6 | 10.1 | 0.7 | 14.8 | 5.7 | 7.5 | 9.3 | 8.8 | 1.7 | 75.7 |
| 4. Quebec | 95.1 | 1.5 | 24.1 | 1.8 | 151.8 | 24.6 | 40.0 | 57.4 | 64.1 | 14.4 | 474.8 |
| 5. Ontario | 209.7 | 1.6 | 31.5 | 19.1 | 254.6 | 51.4 | 71.0 | 83.8 | 100.6 | 22.2 | 845.5 |
| 6. Manitoba | 48.4 | 0.8 | 0.6 | 0.3 | 19.8 | 5.6 | 16.0 | 16.5 | 21.1 | 4.0 | 133.1 |
| 7. Saskatchewan | 74.9 | 0.3 | 0.5 | 0.3 | 3.0 | 0.9 | 13.3 | 11.8 | 13.1 | 3.3 | 121.4 |
| 8. Alberta | 34.0 | 0.2 | 0.7 | 7.4 | 7.2 | 6.3 | 16.2 | 10.5 | 12.6 | 3.6 | 98.7 |
| 9. British Columbia | 11.4 | 6.1 | 11.9 | 13.8 | 32.4 | 14.8 | 27.7 | 18.4 | 20.5 | 8.6 | 165.6 |
| 10. Canada | 513.2 | 20.4 | 86.8 | 58.3 | 507.8 | 115.0 | 203.5 | 223.4 | 254.8 | 61.8 | 2,045.0 |

TABLE B-3

Gross value added (current dollars), by sectors, for provinces, 1929 ($ millions)

| Provinces | Agriculture (1) | Forestry (2) | Fishing and trapping (3) | Mining (4) | Manufacturing (5) | Construction (6) | Transportation (7) | Utilities (8) | Personal and professional services (9) | Domestic trade (10) | Finance (11) | Government (12) | Total 1-12 (13) |
|---|---|---|---|---|---|---|---|---|---|---|---|---|---|
| 1. P.E.I. | 10.0 | 0.1 | 0.9 | — | 2.0 | 0.4 | 4.0 | 0.2 | 3.0 | 2.0 | 2.0 | 1.0 | 25.6 |
| 2. Nova Scotia | 19.0 | 2.0 | 8.0 | 28.0 | 28.0 | 10.0 | 36.0 | 3.0 | 29.0 | 22.0 | 19.0 | 11.0 | 215.0 |
| 3. New Brunswick | 16.0 | 6.0 | 3.0 | 2.0 | 20.0 | 4.0 | 26.0 | 2.0 | 21.0 | 19.0 | 14.0 | 7.0 | 140.0 |
| 4. Quebec | 118.0 | 24.0 | 5.0 | 30.0 | 411.0 | 129.0 | 182.0 | 41.0 | 181.0 | 193.0 | 217.0 | 72.0 | 1,603.0 |
| 5. Ontario | 227.0 | 21.0 | 7.0 | 61.0 | 701.0 | 142.0 | 251.0 | 51.0 | 240.0 | 296.0 | 309.0 | 117.0 | 2,423.0 |
| 6. Manitoba | 54.0 | 2.0 | 3.0 | 2.0 | 49.0 | 25.0 | 57.0 | 6.0 | 48.0 | 61.0 | 57.0 | 18.0 | 382.0 |
| 7. Saskatchewan | 157.0 | 1.0 | 3.0 | 2.0 | 18.0 | 22.0 | 52.0 | 3.0 | 46.0 | 53.0 | 41.0 | 17.0 | 415.0 |
| 8. Alberta | 120.0 | 2.0 | 3.0 | 31.0 | 34.0 | 19.0 | 48.0 | 4.0 | 42.0 | 52.0 | 39.0 | 17.0 | 411.0 |
| 9. British Columbia | 33.0 | 20.0 | 15.0 | 48.0 | 86.0 | 35.0 | 76.0 | 10.0 | 58.0 | 76.0 | 63.0 | 27.0 | 547.0 |
| 10. Canada | 754.0 | 78.1 | 47.9 | 204.0 | 1,349.0 | 386.4 | 732.0 | 120.2 | 668.0 | 774.0 | 761.0 | 287.0 | 6,161.0 |

TABLE B-4

Gross value added (current dollars), by sectors, for provinces, 1956 ($ millions)

| Provinces | Agriculture (1) | Fishing and trapping (2) | Forestry (3) | Mining (4) | Manufacturing (5) | Construction (6) | Transportation (7) | Utilities (8) | Personal and professional services (9) | Domestic trade (10) | Finance (11) | Government (12) | Total 1-12 (13) |
|---|---|---|---|---|---|---|---|---|---|---|---|---|---|
| 1. P.E.I. | 19.0 | 4.0 | — | — | 6.0 | 10.0 | 12.0 | 1.0 | 16.0 | 20.0 | 5.0 | 15.0 | 108.0 |
| 2. Nova Scotia | 28.0 | 25.0 | 16.0 | 50.0 | 160.0 | 86.0 | 110.0 | 18.0 | 145.0 | 145.0 | 46.0 | 145.0 | 974.0 |
| 3. New Brunswick | 38.0 | 8.0 | 46.0 | 12.0 | 125.0 | 79.0 | 102.0 | 13.0 | 85.0 | 108.0 | 35.0 | 55.0 | 706.0 |
| 4. Quebec | 268.0 | 6.0 | 225.0 | 243.0 | 2,888.0 | 759.0 | 649.0 | 171.0 | 737.0 | 923.0 | 506.0 | 391.0 | 7,766.0 |
| 5. Ontario | 491.0 | 11.0 | 126.0 | 246.0 | 4,869.0 | 1,116.0 | 773.0 | 231.0 | 960.0 | 1,365.0 | 803.0 | 741.0 | 11,732.0 |
| 6. Manitoba | 194.0 | 5.0 | 10.0 | 27.0 | 270.0 | 160.0 | 180.0 | 27.0 | 152.0 | 186.0 | 115.0 | 114.0 | 1,440.0 |
| 7. Saskatchewan | 625.0 | 4.0 | 5.0 | 76.0 | 114.0 | 199.0 | 146.0 | 22.0 | 135.0 | 186.0 | 61.0 | 74.0 | 1,647.0 |
| 8. Alberta | 402.0 | 2.0 | 15.6 | 381.0 | 286.0 | 406.0 | 163.0 | 33.0 | 182.0 | 284.0 | 104.0 | 141.0 | 2,399.6 |
| 9. British Columbia | 78.0 | 37.0 | 293.0 | 110.0 | 824.0 | 477.0 | 248.0 | 60.0 | 261.0 | 389.0 | 190.0 | 195.0 | 3,162.0 |
| 10. Canada | 2,143.0 | 102.0 | 736.6 | 1,145.0 | 9,542.0 | 3,292.0 | 2,383.0 | 576.0 | 2,673.0 | 3,606.0 | 1,865.0 | 1,871.0 | 29,934.6 |

the gross output data for each sector as recorded by each province, and the results were totalled to give a national estimate. The latter was then checked against Firestone's original countrywide estimates. Since Firestone's method and sources were used only a brief discussion of the estimating procedure will be given. However, where the method employed to acquire the estimates appearing in Tables B-1-4 differs from Firestone's, a full explanation will be given. Also, for the service sector, a full explanation will be given for the years 1929 and 1956.

AGRICULTURE

The data on agricultural production for 1890 covers only the quantities produced. Values were included starting with the census of 1901 and for all censuses thereafter. For 1890 the census period was the preceding twelve months up to the census date (April 1, 1891), while after 1901 the census year was made to conform to calendar year production, e.g., the 1911 census is an estimate of production for the calendar year 1910.

In 1901 egg production and nursery stock sales were added to the census of agriculture. This procedure was followed in the 1911 census. Also, for both the 1891 and 1911 censuses forest products cut on farms are excluded from the value of agricultural production and are shown in primary forest production.

To estimate the value of agriculture production for 1890 and make it as consistent with the later estimates as possible, it was necessary to break total agricultural production into its component parts, make the appropriate value calculations, then add the results.

*Field Crops*

The agriculture Division of the Dominion Bureau of Statistics made a full set of estimates in 1921 for the value of field crops produced in 1870, 1880, 1890, and 1900. These estimates were first published in the *Monthly Bulletin of Agricultural Statistics*, vol 14, no 153 (May 1921), 200-5. The provincial value figures were obtained by multiplying national prices derived from above by the provincial quantity figures shown in the 1891 census. The effect of interprovincial differences in the *value* of field crop production does not appear in these estimates; only quantity variations are reflected. The value figures for field crops for 1910 are from *Census of Canada, 1911*, vol IV, 358-67 (this also includes value of vegetables produced).

*Fruits and Nursery Stock*

Estimates of the *value* of fruit and nursery production (maple sugar) for 1891 were derived from the values for comparable products which appeared in the

1901 census. The prices prevailing in 1900 were adjusted for the change in prices by the vegetable products price index for 1890 (base 1900 = 100) shown in K. W. Taylor and H. Michell, *Statistical Contributions to Canadian Economic History*, vol II (Toronto, 1931), 56. The 1910 estimates appear in the *Census of Canada, 1911*, vol IV, 368-77. The prices used to estimate values in 1890 are countrywide prices and do not reflect provincial price differences. This is the case in all value estimates for 1890.

### Livestock Slaughtered or Sold for Slaughter or Export

The values of cattle, hogs, and sheep slaughtered on farms or sold for slaughter or export are reported in the *Census of Canada, 1891*, vol IV, 116-221 and *Census of Canada, 1911*, vol IV, 383-9, but value estimates only begin appearing in the 1901 census. The method of estimating value for 1890 is similar to that described for fruits and nursery stock.

### Dairying

The quantities of butter and cheese produced at home, as well as that shipped to butter and cheese manufacturers, were reported in the 1891 and 1911 censuses; values were also given for the latter. Two sources of information were used: the raw material input to the appropriate manufacturing industries, and the census estimates for home production. To obtain value estimates for 1890, the prices for butter and cheese appearing in the 1901 census were projected backward on the basis of the trend in export prices for these products (all calculations were on a per pound basis). The value for dairy production for 1910 was based on the census value estimates for milk production which appear in the 1911 census (vol IV, 400).

### Wool, Honey and Wax, and Eggs

The quantities of these commodities, except eggs, are shown in the 1891 and 1911 censuses, but value figures are available only in 1911. The quantity of production of wool, honey, and wax is shown in *Census of Canada, 1891*, vol IV, 116-231. To obtain value estimates, price per pound in 1900 for each of these commodities was used with these prices extrapolated back to 1890 on the basis of the trend in export prices for these products. This adjusted price was then multiplied by the provincial quantities of production shown in the 1891 census.

Data on egg production were not collected until the 1901 census, which reported both the quantity (vol II, 54-61) and the value (vol II, xxix). The value of egg production in 1890 was estimated by calculating the number of eggs the hens and chickens laid as reported in the 1901 census. This laying rate was then multiplied by the hens and chickens reported on farms and lots for each province to obtain the quantity of production. Price estimates were obtained by extrapolating back to 1890 the 1901 prices, adjusted for changes in the price of eggs exported. This information was obtained from the 1891 and 1901 decennial censuses, especially p. xxix of vol II of the 1901 census. Egg production in 1910 is shown in *Census of Canada, 1911*, vol IV, 400. The data were collected on a provincial basis, as were all of the components of total agricultural production listed above.

## *Duplications and Deductions*

The details of the method used to remove duplication from the gross estimates outlined above are given in Firestone.[3] Briefly, the figure used to deduct the value of materials consumed in production from the value of output was 29.3 per cent. This was found by averaging the amount deducted from the gross value of agricultural production to cover the value of seed used and of feed grain, fodder, and milk fed to livestock for the years 1920 to 1939. These calculations appear in the annual publications of the DBS report, *Survey of Production*, for these years.

## *General Qualifications*

There are at least two main areas of contention in these regional agricultural estimates of gross value added. First is the pricing of agricultural output for 1891. It is obvious that simple extrapolation of export price indexes for a broadly defined collection of similar commodities runs the risk of misrepresenting the "true" prices of these commodities in 1891. Domestic prices can and do differ from international prices, because the number of effective alternative sources of supply are necessarily less than in the international market. In addition, this potential error is compounded even further by applying a national value figure to regional output data. Prices for similar commodities differ between regions, and the deviation is probably greater for earlier periods. Any comments on the exact direction of the biases imbedded in these estimates is impossible at this time.

The second major area of concern is in the application of a single deflator to the gross value series. This deflator attempts to remove the amount of inter-industry flows from the gross value estimates. What is implied here, then, is that this interindustry component remained constant for about three decades. This was undoubtedly not the case. The external purchases by the farming sector were probably less for earlier years. The result of using a constant deflator is to underestimate the "true" value added figure for 1891 and 1911. However, there is no question that the gross output estimates are far from perfect. Thus, the net effect if corrections for both were made is uncertain. Also, as in the discussion of prices, applying a national deflator to the gross value estimates of all provinces is bound to distort somewhat the interregional value added levels from what they would be had regional deflators been available.

The above discussion points out clearly where additional work is required to improve the quality of these data. However, a word in defence of the estimates is in order. The qualifications outlined above operate largely at or near the margin of the main output figures shown in the various censuses. Thus pending the discovery of a new body of data, the type of adjustments discussed above, when all the "plus" changes are grouped with the "minus" ones, will probably not diverge greatly from those shown in this appendix. At a minimum these data as they stand indicate fairly accurately changes in this sector's contribution to regional and national output.

### FISHING AND TRAPPING

The value of primary fishing products for 1890 was estimated from the *Statistical Year Book of Canada, 1891*, 346. For 1911 the data came from the *Census of Canada, 1911*, vol v, p. x. The data for both years were collected for the fiscal year ending in June 1891 and in March 1911. These figures include the total value of fish marketed, whether in fresh, dried, cured, canned, or other prepared state; hence they had to be adjusted to exclude the value added by processing, since this appears in the "manufactures" item. It was estimated in *Fisheries Statistics of Canada* (1917 and on) that between 1917 and 1926 the value of fish caught and landed averaged 63.7 per cent of the total "value of fisheries" figure. This proportion was used to estimate the value of fish caught for 1891 and 1911.

The trapping figures cover the value of furs of wild animals only, as the value of furs taken on fur farms is included in agricultural production. The data for the value of wild fur production for 1891 and 1911 are shown in the *Census of Canada, 1911*, vol v, p. xiii.

It was not felt necessary to reduce these gross figures of production for fish and furs by the amount of input from other sectors, because it was felt such expenses represented only a minor fraction of the total value. However, it is well to note that the estimates are somewhat overvalued as a result.

### MINING

Included in the output of this sector are metallic ores (copper, silver, gold, etc.), abrasives (corundum, etc.), fuel and light materials (coal-bituminous-marketed, natural gas, and petroleum), pigments (e.g., iron oxide), and items such as asbestos, mica, salt, etc. The source of these output data is *Canadian Mineral Statistics, 1604-1956*, reference paper 68, a DBS publication. These data are by province. The metallic ore estimates are for fully manufactured minerals, and therefore a ratio of inputs to total outputs was calculated. This ratio (approximately 50 per cent) was used to "net-out" the interindustry effect on this category. In addition expenditures by the mining industry on explosives, fuel, purchased electricity, freight charges, and insurance were deducted by deflating the "adjusted" gross outputs by 6 per cent. For an explanation of the derivation of this deflator see Firestone (288).

PRIMARY FOREST PRODUCTION

The census estimates for sawlogs and square timber for 1891 were so unreliable that the values had to be estimated by calculating the cost of materials used in the log products industry–sawmills, shingle mills, lath mills, stave mills–and the values of square timber exported for 1891, less the amount of timber imported.[4] This method was also used to estimate these two items for 1910. The value of primary forest production for 1891 was calculated by first deriving the value figures for 1900 and then extending them back to 1891 on the basis of the trend in prices for exports for the particular products.

The basic data for the 1891 estimates came from the *Census of Canada, 1891,* vol IV, 234-47 and vol III (manufactures), and for exports of squared timber from the *Statistical Year Book of Canada, 1891,* 205. For 1910 estimates the primary source was the *Census of Canada, 1911,* vol V, 30, as well as vol III, Table V for the cost of materials in log products industry, and for the balance of forest production from the *Canada Year Book, 1911,* and *1912,* pages 415 and 65, respectively.

Since we were using the input requirements in the log products industry to obtain an estimate of the value of sawlogs produced, it was first necessary to raise the estimates by 1.1 per cent as only firms of five or more hands were included in the 1911 census. Since *all* firms were included in the 1891 census, the adjustment was necesary to make the two estimates comparable.[5] Imports of sawlogs were also removed in order to get an accurate picture of the value of sawlogs produced. It was found that Canadian production amounted to 95.07 per cent of total input into the log products industry.[6]

The values of square timber produced in 1891 and 1911 were estimated by using the export figures for this product for the census years under study. Their provincial production levels were estimated by dividing the total exports by the provincial distribution of other forest production output levels.

Estimates of Firewood Production for 1911 appear in the *Census of Canada, 1911,* vol V, Table III. Only quantity estimates are available for 1891 (vol IV, 492), so the value estimates reported in vol II, lxii of the 1901 census were used and extrapolated back to 1891 on the basis of the trend in export prices for these commodities. In the case of Pulpwood Production, the 1891 estimates came from the quantity production figures of the *Census of Canada, 1891,* vol IV, and their values were calculated similarly to those of firewood. The 1911 esti- mates on the other hand were collected from the *Canada Year Book, 1911,* 415. Shingles and Lath output data were taken, for 1890, from the *Census of Canada, 1891,* vol IV, 493, and for 1910 from the *Canada Year Book, 1912,* 65 (these are for 1911 production and so probably overstate slightly the true 1910 values).

The balance of the products included in primary forest production, e.g., spars for masts, tan bark, railway ties, sleepers, electric light and telegraph poles, mining timbers, etc., was obtained from the *Census of Canada, 1891*, vol IV, 492 for 1890, and from the *Canada Year Book, 1912*, for 1910.

As noted at the beginning of this appendix the estimates for 1929 and 1956 were obtained from the *Survey of Production, 1961*. This publication, unfortunately, does not carry the value added revisions for the forest products industry back to 1929. Thus, the estimates used for the provinces were those given in the *Canada Year Book, 1932*, 173. Since they appeared to be greatly overstated when compared with the revised series starting in 1935 and shown in the 1961 issue of *Survey of Production*, p. 21, it was decided to reduce the former estimate by the proportional difference between this estimate and that given in *National Accounts Income and Expenditure, 1926-56*, 56, for gross domestic product in the forest industry. The difference was apportioned on the basis of provincial distribution of net value added in the primary forest industry as it appeared in the *Canada Year Book, 1936*. The difference was approximately 25 per cent.

MANUFACTURING

The basic sources of the data for 1890 and 1910 are the appropriate decennial censuses (vol III in each case). These censuses list, by establishment, the gross value of production and the major expenses incurred in production. Value added by manufacturing, then, is the gross value of production less these costs of materials and supplies consumed in the production process and less expenditures for services included under the services category. The value of output shown in the *Census of Canada, 1911*, vol III, Table I, covers only establishments with five or more employees. This is in contrast to the enumeration of manufacturers shown in vol III, p. 382 of the 1891 census which includes all establishments, regardless of size. To make the two series comparable it was necessary to increase both the gross value of output and the cost of materials by the amount of undercoverage for 1910. The 1911 census appears to have covered only 92.2 per cent,[7] and the recorded values were raised accordingly. This adjustment factor was the same for all provinces. Since it would be assumed that smaller establishments predominate on the frontier, the manufacturing value added estimates for 1911 for these regions are probably an underestimate of the true value. Also, in 1911 the expense incurred by manufacturing establishments in purchasing electricity was not included in the census enumeration. To allow for this deficit an amount equal to half the total value of all purchased electricity was estimated as expenses incurred by the manufacturing industries.[8] Adjustments for fuel and electricity for the 1890 manufacturing output were based on the percentage these figures represented to total output for 1900 (1.47 per cent).

The last adjustment made was for expenditure on other materials and services included in manufacturing production, e.g., packages, cartons, and shipping containers, office supplies, and materials for plant and equipment. For 1890 the deduction from gross value was 5 per cent, while for 1910 it was 6 per cent.[9]

CONSTRUCTION

Since the decennial censuses of 1891 and 1911 did not report the value of construction work during the census periods, the required estimates were derived by estimating the values of the flow of construction materials to this industry and raising them to cover the total cost of construction work. The available supply of construction materials is the value of domestic production plus imports, including the duty, minus exports. The cost of materials was estimated at 51.6 per cent of the total value of work performed.[10] The material expenditure totals were then raised by this amount. Again this adjustment figure was used for all provinces.

The basic source for information on construction materials used in 1911 was the *Census of Canada*, vols III and V, which contained the necessary information on the values of such primary forest construction products as railway ties, fence posts, telephone poles, etc. The latter volume gave estimates of wood products of higher manufacture used in construction, e.g., lath, shingles, etc. (here only the value added of the establishments producing these materials was used in order to avoid duplication with the forest products industry). Also derived from the census of manufacturers (vol III, Table V) was the value of electric apparatus. These data were supplemented by information on values of structural minerals and mineral products in *Chronological Record of Canadian Mining Events, 1604 to 1947*, a DBS publication. The data for 1891 came from the *Census of Canada, 1891*, vol III. The exports and imports of construction materials were taken from the *Statistical Year Book of Canada, 1891*, 158-59 and the *Canada Year Book, 1911*, Tables XXVI and XXX. They were apportioned provincially on the basis of the distribution of domestic production of the materials.

The value of lumber (log figures were reduced by 72.1 per cent to conform with the estimated construction use of this product), fence posts and poles (main source *Canada Year Book, 1911*, 414), and structural materials–net value, and the value of iron and steel products used in construction (for calculation of this estimate see Firestone, 295)–was totalled and raised (divided by 51.6 per cent, see above) to obtain the total value of construction. From this total was subtracted the total value added by the construction trades, which was included in the manufacturing value added (vols III of both the 1891 and 1911 censuses). The result, calculated for each province, gave an estimate of the net value of construction for the census periods of 1891 and 1911. In retrospect it would appear that the estimates are below their true value, especially in areas, such as the prairies, which had to import the majority of their construction materials. To obtain the value for such areas would require detailed knowledge of the interprovincial transfer of construction materials. Since this type of information is not available, an overestimate of construction value added occurred in regions, such as Ontario, Quebec, British Columbia, and New Brunswick, which are large producers of construction materials.

SERVICE INDUSTRIES

Service industries comprise transportation, storage, communication, public utilities, wholesale and retail trade, finance, insurance, and real estate operations as well as personal and business services. For 1890 and 1910 the values added were based on samples (for a definition see below). The samples covered the value added per person in personal and domestic service and in transportation, and the services of doctors, dentists, clergymen, and professors. The value added for the balance of the service sector was estimated by multiplying the number of workers in each occupation by a composite value added per worker. This composite multiplier was derived by taking a value mid-way between the average value added per worker in the commodity sector and the value added per worker in the sample group in the service sector. These average values added per worker were computed for the country as a whole and were applied to the nine provinces. Thus, provincial differences in value added per worker were not incorporated in the results. However, differences in the number of employees in these industries among provinces were taken into account.

The first step was to acquire a series of employment in the service industries that was consistent between the two census years.[11] Next the value added estimates for the sample group were obtained. For transportation the net earnings plus total wages of steam railways was used (*Canada Year Book, 1911*, 354-57). Domestic and personal service estimates are from Firestone, 261. The estimates of numbers in the professional group for 1911 were taken directly from the *Census of Canada, 1911*, vol VI. For 1891, the numbers of professionals were taken from *Census of Canada, 1891*, vol II, and earnings were obtained by extrapolating back those registered in the *Census of Canada, 1901*: *Earnings by Occupations Bulletin 1*, 79, on the basis of an index for domestic and municipal employees, found in the *Board of Inquiry into Cost of Living in Canada, 1915*, vol II, 430. The same procedure was used for 1911. The earnings of this sample group (transportation, domestics, doctors, dentists, clergy, and teachers) were averaged for 1891 and 1911, and the difference between these figures and the average value added for the commodity group for the respective census years was estimated. This "computed" value added per worker was then multiplied by the number of employees in each of the remaining occupations included under the service industries.[12]

The 1891 estimate of the value added by service industries for Canada was found to be significantly different from that recorded by Firestone–$271 million, while Firestone's figure was $214 million. The difference arises from the distribution of workers among occupations. Firestone apparently uses the occupational distribution of workers given in the 1891 census (vol III), while I use an "adjusted" series comprised of a distribution by industry. The redistribution involves mainly labourers and office clerks and is based on their industrial attachment in 1911.[13] With the greater number of employees listed in occupations such as transportation, municipal employees, etc., it is natural for my estimate to exceed Firestone's.

The estimates of the service industries' value added for 1929 and 1956 were derived principally from the 1931 and 1951 censuses and the appropriate *Canada Year Book*. To simplify the exposition of the method used, the approach to measuring value added will be given for each of the main component industries.

### Transportation and Communication

The approach in this case was to use the total revenue earned by the railways and truck systems and the telephone and telegraph companies. Since the accepted method of deriving such estimates is to total the costs incurred by these industries in providing their services (e.g., wages, interest, rent, etc.), the estimates for 1929 and 1956 are an overstatement of the true value added for this group of industries. For example, in the case of railways expenses amounted to 95 per cent of the revenue earned. Revenue figures were used since it was possible to obtain them in more series than was the case for expense items. The main sources for these estimates were the *Canada Year Book, 1934-35*, 704 ff, and *1959,* ch. XVIII. These totals were for Canada only, however, and so it was necessary to distribute them by province. This was done on the basis of the provincial distribution of the labour force engaged in this industry. This latter distribution was taken from the 1931 and 1951 censuses of the industrial distribution of the labour force.[14]

### Domestic Trade

The basic approach for the wholesale and retail trades involved an attempt to remove, from the sales figures given for these industries, any interindustry duplications. This meant, primarily, the elimination of the "cost of goods" sold plus other interindustry purchases. This approach was used for the 1956 estimates. In the *Census of Canada, 1951*, vols VII and VIII appears a record of sales (i.e., gross sales less cost of goods) for the retail and wholesale trades, by provinces. It was necessary, then, to calculate the gross margin earned on net sales. Gross margin is the total of net profits, salaries, and other expenses. The percentage of gross margin to net sales was obtained in a biennial survey of the retail and wholesale trades. This survey started in 1946. Gross sales figures, by province, appear annually in the various issues of the *Canada Year Book*.

To calculate the value added of domestic trade the net sales figures from the census of 1951 were multiplied for each province, by an index of gross sales figures (1951 = 100). Then these adjusted net sales figures, in this case for 1956, were reduced by a figure representing the average, for all types of wholesale and retail stores, of the percentage of gross margin to net sales. In this case these percentages appear in the *Canada Year Book, 1958-59*, 905 ff. Gross margins for both the retail and wholesale trades were available. These gross margins, however, are for the country as a whole, and so they do not show interprovincial differences.

The retail and wholesale value added figures for 1929 were taken directly from appendix 4 of the *Rowell-Serois Commission on Dominion-Provincial Affairs*, "National Income." These data appear on a provincial basis.

## Government

The government, for the purpose of a production account, is considered to be a producer of services such as public administration, defence, education, and health. These services are valued as cost and are shown as if they were purchased by governments. Thus, the value added by the government is represented by the total of wages and salaries paid to government employees and military pay and allowances. Also included here, since they could not be successfully eliminated, were defence services and mutual aid as well as general government expenses (e.g., office expenses). The figures are for the fiscal year ending March 31 and include federal, provincial, and municipal expenses. The estimates of these expenditures appeared in *National Accounts Income and Expenditure, 1926-56*, Table 43. The data, however, appeared on a Canada-wide basis and had to be distributed provincially. This was done on the basis of the provincial distribution of employees attached to the government sector as shown in the 1931 and 1951 censuses.

## Finance

The two industries included in this subsector are the chartered banks and the insurance companies. To show their contribution to total product, we merely totalled the revenue earned by these firms, since the product produced is wholly a service. However, total earnings were not reported before 1951. Thus, we used the average ratio of net profits to current earnings for the years 1951 to 1955 to inflate the net profit figures shown for 1929. The basic data for these estimates appear in the *Canada Year Book, 1959*, chapters XXIV and XXV, and *1934-35*, chapters XII and XIII. Again, the revenue figures were only collected on an nationwide basis. They were distributed to the provinces by the provincial distribution of employees listed as working in these industries shown in the 1931 and 1951 censuses.

## Professional and Personal Service

Included in this group are domestic service employees, caretakers, etc., as well as lawyers, doctors, etc. Their contribution was estimated by taking the total of wages and salaries accruing to them. These figures appear in the *Census of Canada, 1951*, vol v, Table 24 and the *Census of Canada, 1931*, vol v, Table 27. To extrapolate these estimates to 1956 and 1929, respectively, national indices of earnings and employment for the broad category of professional and personal services were used. These indices are from the *Canada Year Book, 1961*, 737, and *1931*, 778. Since these indices are for national movements, the assumption here is that all the provincial trends in service employment and wages followed a similar trend.

RECONCILIATION OF PROVINCIAL GROSS VALUE ADDED ESTIMATES

It is necessary to reconcile the estimates derived here with extant data. Unfortunately no direct comparison is possible, even for the most recent period. The only provincial estimates available are those for personal income by province. As mentioned in chapter one, the personal income approach is not directly comparable to the value added method (the former, by definition, is always less than the latter). However, the official series provide some basis for judging whether our estimates approximate the correct orders of magnitude in the last two years measured (1929 and 1956). Probably the best comparison is the percentage distribution of income and output among the provinces. The comparison shows that the gross value added method, even though calculated differently from the income approach, presents a good representation of provincial levels of performance. Although this does not prove that the GVA estimates derived here

TABLE B-5

A comparison of official estimates of total personal income with gross value added estimates, by province, 1929 and 1956

| Provinces | Personal income (millions of current dollars) | | | | Gross value added (millions of current dollars) | | | |
|---|---|---|---|---|---|---|---|---|
| | 1929 | Per cent | 1956 | Per cent | 1929 | Per cent | 1956 | Per cent |
| | (1) | (2) | (3) | (4) | (5) | (6) | (7) | (8) |
| 1. P.E.I. | 24 | 0.5 | 78 | 0.4 | 26 | 0.4 | 108 | 0.4 |
| 2. Nova Scotia | 169 | 3.7 | 675 | 3.1 | 215 | 3.5 | 974 | 3.2 |
| 3. New Brunswick | 121 | 2.7 | 497 | 2.3 | 140 | 2.3 | 706 | 2.4 |
| 4. Quebec | 1,163 | 25.4 | 5,318 | 24.7 | 1,603 | 26.0 | 7,766 | 25.9 |
| 5. Ontario | 1,873 | 40.6 | 8,617 | 40.1 | 2,423 | 39.5 | 11,732 | 39.2 |
| 6. Manitoba | 303 | 6.6 | 1,126 | 5.2 | 382 | 6.2 | 1,440 | 4.8 |
| 7. Saskatchewan | 271 | 5.7 | 1,226 | 5.7 | 415 | 6.7 | 1,647 | 5.5 |
| 8. Alberta | 290 | 6.3 | 1,635 | 7.6 | 411 | 6.6 | 2,400 | 8.0 |
| 9. British Columbia | 394 | 8.5 | 2,332 | 10.8 | 547 | 8.8 | 3,162 | 10.6 |
| 10. Canada | 4,608 | 100.0 | 21,504 | 100.0 | 6,162 | 100.0 | 29,935 | 100.0 |

SOURCE:   Cols 1 and 3: *National Accounts Income and Expenditure, 1926-56*, 64; Cols 5 and 7: Tables B-3 and B-4.

are without fault, it does demonstrate that confidence can be placed in them to indicate the relative positions of provinces and to outline the differential growth rates among regions.

A comparison of the 1890 and 1910 gross value added estimates with other series is impossible. To the author's knowledge no other regional estimates based on the province as the unit of study have been made for the years prior to 1926. The best that can be done is to compare the national totals derived from summing the provincial estimates with Firestone's original national estimates. This will simply indicate whether our regional estimates are approximating total economic activity in Canada, but such a test in no way proves that the provincial estimates represent the true levels of output.

The comparison of regional totals with the national estimates is shown in Table B-6.

---

TABLE B-6

A comparison of Firestone's estimates of GNP, with national GVA summed from provincial estimates, 1890 and 1910

|  | Firestone's estimate of GNP | National GVA based on provincial estimates |
|---|---|---|
|  | (1) | (2) |
|  | (millions of current dollars) | |
| 1. 1890 | 734 | 793 |
| 2. 1910 | 2048 | 2044 |

SOURCE AND METHOD: Col 1: O. J. Firestone, *Canada's Economic Development, 1867-1953*, Income and Wealth Series VII (London, 1958), 281. These totals are for the commodity-producing and service industries only. Col 2: Tables B-1 and B-2.

---

The largest deviation occurs for the 1890 estimate. An explanation for part of this discrepancy was given earlier in appendix B (see the notes on estimating output for the service industries).

Although the general agreement between these two national figures is no assurance of provincial level accuracy, two observations about the latter can be made. First, the methods used to estimate provincial GVA for 1890 and 1910 are, in most respects, the same as used in obtaining the 1929 and 1956 figures. Second, trends in output change agree very closely with trends in labour force change in total and by sector (see Tables III-5 and III-6). Since the former, with the exception of parts of the service industry, were derived independently of the latter it would appear that they represent closely the levels of, and changes in, provincial output. All quantitative estimates, including those presented in this appendix, contain elements of subjective valuation. The extent of the intrusion of the latter type of decision increases as earlier estimates are attempted. Careful evaluation, therefore, should be made before the suggestions are pushed too far.

*Estimation of Real Value Added*

The provincial gross value added estimates presented in Tables B-1, B-2, B-3, and B-4 are in current dollar totals. Since our main concern is with long-term changes, it is necessary to separate growth in real final product from growth in output which is attributable solely to price movements. To obtain a deflated series, the current dollar values were divided by a consumer's price index with a base constructed of prices averaged over the years 1935-39. This particular base was chosen because the well-known negative correlation between proportional changes in quantities and prices means that an index with an 1890 base would overestimate real growth, while a base for 1956 would understate growth in real output. Thus a base in the middle range of our estimates was selected in order to minimize these upward and downward biases, and an attempt was made to maintain as much comparability as possible with existing national estimates of real income, e.g., those prepared by Firestone (317-18). Since this index ended in 1953, it was necessary to splice his 1935-39 base to the implicit index for gross national product shown in the *National Accounts, 1926-56*, 36.

A single price deflator such as this has two basic deficiencies. By deflating both the provincial and national output estimates with the same index, differences in price variations among provinces are not represented. Although the biases so created are assumed to be minor, they nevertheless must be kept in mind. No consideration is given here to differential price trends between the sectors: price changes for A sector goods are assumed to move in a similar fashion with those in the other two sectors. Only more detailed study of sector price trends will demonstrate the biases in our real output estimates created by the single CPI deflator.[15]

Estimates of gross value added in constant dollars, by provinces for the four years under review are given in Table B-7.

TABLE B-7

GVA (1935-9 prices), by provinces, selected years, 1890-1956

| Provinces | 1890 | 1910 | 1929 | 1956 |
|---|---|---|---|---|
| P.E.I. | 22.80 | 21.45 | 21.48 | 53.77 |
| Nova Scotia | 103.20 | 154.71 | 180.37 | 484.87 |
| New Brunswick | 78.99 | 102.63 | 117.45 | 351.45 |
| Quebec | 336.00 | 644.07 | 1,344.80 | 3,865.99 |
| Ontario | 629.58 | 1,147.26 | 2,032.72 | 5,840.30 |
| Manitoba | 48.92 | 180.53 | 320.47 | 716.85 |
| Saskatchewan | 15.39 | 164.72 | 348.15 | 819.89 |
| Alberta | (a) | 133.65 | 344.80 | 1,194.25 |
| British Columbia | 42.05 | 224.64 | 458.89 | 1,574.07 |
| Canada | 1,276.92 | 2,773.66 | 5,169.13 | 14,901.43 |

# APPENDIX C
# Labour Force Estimates

THE LABOUR FORCE includes all persons who, during the week ending with the census, were gainfully occupied and were over the age of fourteen in the case of the 1951 census and ten and over in the case of the 1891, 1911, and 1931 censuses.[1] A person gainfully occupied, in census usage, is one who pursues an occupation and earns money or money equivalents. Thus, persons not so engaged are considered as being outside the labour force. Of this latter group an important part belongs to unpaid family workers, mainly on farms. The early censuses specifically exclude such persons if they are simultaneously attending school,[2] while in the 1951 census unpaid family workers are excluded, whether or not they attend school.[3]

Persons in the labour force were classified by occupation and by industries in the 1951, 1931, and 1911 censuses but only by occupations for the 1891 census. The industrial classification of workers was used as far as possible, throughout the thesis.[4]

To extrapolate the census data of 1931 and 1951 to the appropriate years (1929 and 1956), indexes of employment, showing the annual changes in labour force by main industry groupings, were used. The indexes for the 1929 and 1956 estimates are given in the *Canada Year Book* of 1932 and 1959, p. 653 and p. 732, respectively. However, these employment by industry indexes were for Canada as a whole, the assumption in such a calculation being that all provincial industries grew at the same rate as the national averages. This obviously creates some errors. In the case of agriculture, however, where annual provincial figures are available, the estimates were found to agree quite closely with the estimated totals.

In the 1891 labour force estimates, it was found necessary to rearrange the presentation given in the census report, because the original data were not differentiated by occupation. The classification process used was that adopted in the 1931 census, vol VII, Table 54. This particular classification was used because it served as the basis for subsequent reclassifications for the 1901, 1911, and 1921 censuses and has been used in the 1941 and 1951 censuses. The reclassification of the 1891 census of occupations was done for all provinces.

To place this new occupational classification more on a footing with the industrial classifications of 1911, 1929, and 1956 estimates, the undifferentiated categories of clerks and labourers were distributed to their specific groups on the basis of their distribution in the 1911 census.[5] It is this redistribution that causes the estimates of the service industries' value added for 1891 to differ from that of Firestone's.[6] For example, it was found that by far the largest share of labourers belonged in the transportation category. The result was to inflate this group from 63,975 to 76,348, while the majority of the clerks, mainly females, were reallocated to the government sector.

TABLE C-1

Gainfully occupied by sectors, for provinces, 1891 (thousands)

| Provinces | Agriculture (1) | Fishing and trapping (2) | Forestry (3) | Mining (4) | Manufacturing (5) | Construction (6) | Transportation (7) | Personal and professional services (8) | Domestic trade (9) | Government (10) | Total 1-10 (11) |
|---|---|---|---|---|---|---|---|---|---|---|---|
| 1. P.E.I. | 21.8 | 0.9 | 0.1 | — | 4.1 | 2.1 | 0.5 | 3.8 | 1.3 | 0.4 | 35.0 |
| 2. Nova Scotia | 61.4 | 14.6 | 1.5 | 7.4 | 22.1 | 9.7 | 9.4 | 20.4 | 7.3 | 2.7 | 156.5 |
| 3. New Brunswick | 51.2 | 3.0 | 1.3 | 0.5 | 18.7 | 7.3 | 5.7 | 12.0 | 5.7 | 1.8 | 107.2 |
| 4. Quebec | 207.3 | 4.3 | 4.2 | 3.0 | 83.9 | 36.8 | 20.6 | 46.5 | 31.3 | 11.7 | 449.6 |
| 5. Ontario | 337.5 | 2.5 | 4.2 | 3.4 | 144.5 | 50.4 | 33.3 | 82.4 | 49.3 | 17.2 | 724.7 |
| 6. Manitoba | 34.4 | 0.2 | 0.1 | — | 4.1 | 3.1 | 2.4 | 4.3 | 3.7 | 1.4 | 53.7 |
| 7. Saskatchewan | 13.2 | 0.2 | 0.1 | — | 1.1 | 1.2 | 1.2 | 1.7 | 0.9 | 1.5 | 21.1 |
| 8. Alberta | (a) | (a) | (a) | (a) | (c) | (a) | (a) | (a) | (a) | (a) | (a) |
| 9. British Columbia | 8.3 | 4.5 | 1.4 | 5.2 | 9.3 | 4.8 | 3.3 | 5.6 | 3.1 | 2.2 | 47.7 |
| 10. Canada | 735.1 | 30.2 | 12.9 | 19.5 | 287.8 | 115.4 | 76.4 | 176.7 | 102.6 | 38.9 | 1,595.5 |

NOTE: (a) Alberta and the Northwest Territories were included with the Saskatchewan returns.

TABLE C-2

Gainfully occupied by sectors, for provinces, 1911 (thousands)

| Provinces | Agriculture (1) | Fishing and trapping (2) | Forestry (3) | Mining (4) | Manufacturing (5) | Construction (6) | Transportation (7) | Personal and professional services (8) | Domestic trade (9) | Government (10) | Total 1-10 (11) |
|---|---|---|---|---|---|---|---|---|---|---|---|
| 1. P.E.I. | 19.8 | 1.4 | 0.1 | — | 2.6 | 1.7 | 1.1 | 3.2 | 1.9 | 0.3 | 32.1 |
| 2. Nova Scotia | 48.7 | 14.7 | 3.2 | 17.1 | 26.1 | 12.6 | 11.4 | 21.1 | 13.7 | 4.7 | 173.3 |
| 3. New Brunswick | 45.7 | 2.9 | 4.4 | 0.8 | 20.2 | 11.8 | 8.0 | 14.2 | 9.8 | 2.1 | 119.9 |
| 4. Quebec | 204.6 | 4.4 | 11.3 | 5.6 | 141.9 | 67.8 | 42.8 | 85.8 | 71.2 | 17.8 | 653.2 |
| 5. Ontario | 307.0 | 3.7 | 10.6 | 16.9 | 230.7 | 83.3 | 76.0 | 123.5 | 111.8 | 27.5 | 991.0 |
| 6. Manitoba | 69.9 | 0.4 | 0.3 | 0.9 | 17.7 | 18.6 | 17.1 | 24.8 | 23.4 | 5.0 | 178.1 |
| 7. Saskatchewan | 133.0 | 1.8 | 0.5 | 0.7 | 7.6 | 14.3 | 14.2 | 17.8 | 14.7 | 4.1 | 208.7 |
| 8. Alberta | 80.5 | 0.9 | 0.7 | 5.2 | 9.6 | 12.2 | 17.3 | 16.9 | 14.0 | 4.5 | 161.8 |
| 9. British Columbia | 24.5 | 4.6 | 11.8 | 15.6 | 35.0 | 24.1 | 29.6 | 27.5 | 22.7 | 10.7 | 206.1 |
| 10. Canada | 933.7 | 34.8 | 42.9 | 62.8 | 491.4 | 246.4 | 217.5 | 334.8 | 283.2 | 76.7 | 2,724.2 |

TABLE C-3

Gainfully occupied by sectors, for provinces, 1929 (thousands)

| Provinces | Agriculture (1) | Forestry, fishing, and trapping (2) | Mining (3) | Manufacturing (4) | Construction (5) | Transportation (6) | Personal and professional services and government (7) | Domestic trade (8) | Utilities (9) | Finance (10) | Total 1-10 (11) |
|---|---|---|---|---|---|---|---|---|---|---|---|
| 1. P.E.I. | 18.4 | 2.8 | — | 1.8 | 1.2 | 1.7 | 4.7 | 2.2 | 0.1 | 0.3 | 33.2 |
| 2. Nova Scotia | 45.1 | 29.7 | 18.9 | 23.3 | 11.2 | 17.4 | 33.3 | 15.5 | 0.9 | 2.6 | 197.9 |
| 3. New Brunswick | 46.5 | 16.2 | 1.2 | 19.3 | 6.8 | 12.8 | 24.7 | 12.3 | 0.5 | 2.0 | 142.3 |
| 4. Quebec | 228.7 | 48.6 | 9.2 | 258.4 | 80.9 | 87.4 | 230.9 | 101.5 | 5.8 | 30.6 | 1,082.0 |
| 5. Ontario | 303.3 | 33.9 | 21.1 | 368.3 | 90.4 | 120.8 | 280.9 | 152.1 | 9.5 | 43.5 | 1,423.8 |
| 6. Manitoba | 92.1 | 9.9 | 2.4 | 32.5 | 15.6 | 27.3 | 55.6 | 31.9 | 1.5 | 8.0 | 276.8 |
| 7. Saskatchewan | 198.5 | 5.1 | 0.9 | 11.3 | 11.8 | 24.8 | 54.3 | 22.3 | 0.7 | 5.8 | 335.5 |
| 8. Alberta | 139.4 | 5.7 | 12.3 | 17.0 | 10.6 | 23.1 | 49.9 | 22.3 | 0.7 | 5.6 | 286.6 |
| 9. British Columbia | 41.9 | 52.7 | 14.2 | 54.9 | 24.4 | 36.5 | 67.8 | 35.5 | 1.2 | 8.8 | 337.9 |
| 10. Canada | 1,113.9 | 204.6 | 80.2 | 786.8 | 252.9 | 351.8 | 802.1 | 395.6 | 20.9 | 107.2 | 4,116.0 |

## TABLE C-4
### Labour force, by sectors, for provinces, 1956 (thousands)

| Provinces | Agriculture (1) | Fishing and trapping (2) | Forestry (3) | Mining (4) | Manufacturing (5) | Construction (6) | Transportation (7) | Utilities (8) | Personal and professional service and government (9) | Domestic trade (10) | Finance (11) | Total 1-11 (12) |
|---|---|---|---|---|---|---|---|---|---|---|---|---|
| 1. P.E.I. | 12.9 | 1.7 | 0.2 | — | 3.8 | 2.2 | 2.3 | 0.3 | 8.1 | 4.6 | 0.5 | 36.6 |
| 2. Nova Scotia | 23.2 | 9.8 | 4.8 | 17.2 | 39.5 | 19.5 | 20.2 | 3.1 | 66.2 | 35.1 | 4.2 | 242.8 |
| 3. New Brunswick | 26.7 | 4.5 | 13.2 | 1.3 | 33.3 | 12.0 | 18.5 | 2.0 | 39.7 | 26.0 | 3.2 | 180.4 |
| 4. Quebec | 193.7 | 5.2 | 36.9 | 22.0 | 484.1 | 121.9 | 118.7 | 15.3 | 352.1 | 202.2 | 46.1 | 1,598.2 |
| 5. Ontario | 206.4 | 2.4 | 19.3 | 34.8 | 677.3 | 156.0 | 145.6 | 38.5 | 471.1 | 321.6 | 75.2 | 2,148.2 |
| 6. Manitoba | 73.3 | 1.6 | 1.2 | 4.4 | 52.3 | 20.3 | 32.8 | 4.2 | 72.2 | 55.6 | 10.5 | 328.4 |
| 7. Saskatchewan | 146.9 | 1.4 | 0.6 | 1.9 | 19.9 | 13.7 | 26.6 | 2.2 | 65.1 | 39.8 | 5.6 | 323.7 |
| 8. Alberta | 114.4 | 1.0 | 1.4 | 17.3 | 38.1 | 30.5 | 29.9 | 4.1 | 86.6 | 54.7 | 9.4 | 387.4 |
| 9. British Columbia | 27.5 | 4.8 | 20.4 | 12.6 | 109.8 | 30.5 | 45.3 | 5.8 | 126.5 | 82.5 | 17.3 | 483.0 |
| 10. Canada | 825.0 | 32.4 | 98.0 | 111.5 | 1,458.1 | 406.6 | 439.9 | 75.5 | 1,287.6 | 822.1 | 172.0 | 5,728.7 |

# NOTES

CHAPTER ONE

1 R. D. Howland, *Some Regional Aspects of Canada's Economic Development,* Royal Commission on Canada's Economic Prospects (Ottawa, 1957), 13.

2 Other omitted items are corporation profit taxes, withholding taxes, government investment income, adjustment on grain transactions, inventory valuation, and employer and employee contributions to social insurance and government pension funds. Dominion Bureau of Statistics, *National Accounts Income and Expenditure, 1960* (Ottawa, 1961), 23.

3 "Farm and Urban Purchasing Power," *Studies in Income and Wealth,* vol xi (New York, 1949), 153-78.

4 Unweighted results are used in this discussion of range differentials to make the results conform to the international results, which were also unweighted.

5 S. Kuznets, "Quantitative Aspects of the Economic Growth of Nations," in *Economic Development and Cultural Change,* vol v, no 1 (October 1956), Table 4, 17.

6 S. Kuznets, "Industrial Distribution of Income and Labour Force by States, United States, 1919-21 to 1955," in *Economic Development and Cultural Change,* vol vi, no 4, part ii (July 1958), 7. This range covers grouped states.

7 In this study we are concerned only with the levels of association between income and other economic variables and not their absolute values.

8 For example, in Canada it was estimated that males earn on the average twice as much as women. Howland, *Some Regional Aspects of Canada's Economic Development,* 238.

9 The average earnings used were those covering the twelve-month period from June 1, 1930, to June 1, 1931. These earnings appeared in the 1931 census and were used because similar averages in the 1941 census appear to understate the average earnings of young males. Average earnings were not reported in the 1951 census.

10 A direct comparison between regional ranges in the shares of the A and M sectors within Canada and the differences observed between countries for recent years shows that within Canada the share range (highest divided by lowest) for the A sector is approximately 7 to 1, while internationally the range between the top 19 and bottom 22 countries is about 3 to 1. For the M sector the interprovincial range is 3 to 1, while the international range is 2.3 to 1. In both sectors interregional exceed international ranges, but we know that the interregional income range for 1956 (Table I-1) is only 2 to 1, while internationally it is 15 to 1. This finding implies that, with lower income differences within Canada, the structure of demand is probably more similar than between countries, and, with the higher spatial concentration of economic activity intranationally, we can presume that a relatively greater weight of internal trade to regional output takes place than of

foreign trade relative to total output for most national units. For a fuller discussion of these relationships see Kuznets, "Industrial Distribution of Income and Labour Force by States, United States, 1919-21 to 1955," 12-16.

11 In low income (or, in an international comparison, less developed countries) areas it has been suggested that the high shares of output and labour force in the S sector are the result of population pressure on the land and the limitations of employment in the M sector. Failure of the latter to grow may be due to a small local market, foreign competition, or capital scarcity. Thus, pressure is exerted on the labour force to seek jobs in service employment. In the rich regions, on the other hand, the growth in S sector is related to increasing productivity in the A and M sectors, which releases labour from them. This "supply" condition is coupled with a rise in demand for S sector services from these two sections, since at higher levels of technology and urbanization the demand for an educated population and labour force plus the generally greater complexity of the economic system at advanced stages of development means more demand on government services. In addition the income elasticity of demand for services is high, thus consumer demand is high. There is obviously a world of difference between the factors inducing S sector expansion in high income and low income areas. See Simon Kuznets, *Six Lectures on Economic Growth* (Glencoe, Illinois, 1959), 60-66.

12 *Ibid.*, Table 6, 50-51.

13 Total personal income was used in this calculation because it more closely approximated gross value added than did service income.

14 The weighted inequality in gross value added per worker is identical to that of total personal income per worker.

15 The magnitude of intersectoral differences depends partly on the number sectors considered. Thus, given a set of interprovincial differences, the intersectoral component within them will be proportionately greater the greater the sector detail, all other conditions being equal.

CHAPTER TWO

1 This is a vague phrase and one hard to define. It implies a sudden change in the structure of the economy from resource to non-resource orientation: a rise in the share of secondary manufacturing industries brought about by changes in economies of scale. The existence of such a "break" or "kink" in Canadian development would be hard to prove. However, 1910 or the years immediately after do signify the end of frontier settlement as it was observed in the first decade of this century, and certainly since 1910 the internal market in Canada has expanded, so permitting some import substitution. A more complete description of general economic change before and after 1910 is given in chapter four. For a fuller discussion of judging national "maturity" see R. E. Caves and R. H. Holton, *The Canadian Economy* (Cambridge, Mass., 1961), 60-78.

2 S. Kuznets, *Modern Economic Growth* (New Haven, 1966), 63.

3 For example, D. J. Daly, chart 2, shows distinct variations in the growth rates of immigration as a percentage of total population. Peaks occurred in 1884, 1912, 1927, and 1956; troughs in 1895, 1917, and 1941. D. J. Daly "Long Cycles and Recent Canadian Experience," *Royal Commission on Banking And Finance*, vol 2, appendix, 279-301.

4 S. Kuznets and R. Goldsmith, *Income and Wealth of the United States Trends and Structure*, Income and Wealth Series II (Cambridge, 1952), 73.

5 O. I. Firestone, *Canada's Economic Development 1867-1953*, Income and Wealth Series VII (London, 1958), 222.

6 *Ibid.*, Table 81, 223.

7 For a discussion of the role of education in improving labour force quality see Gordon W. Bertram, *The Contribution of Education to Economic Growth*, Staff Study 12, Economic Council of Canada (Ottawa, 1966).

8 However, the actual contribution of such age-sex shifts in the United States are thought to be small. Edward F. Denison, *The Sources of Economic Growth in the United States*, Committee for Economic Development (1962), 83.

9 More precisely, the unweighted index of regional population inequality, $\Delta$, is

$$\Delta = \sum \left| \frac{\dfrac{L_x}{L_x}}{N} - \frac{\sum \dfrac{L_x}{\Sigma L_x}}{N} \right|,$$

where   $L_x$ = number of males or females in a given age group in a province,
$\Sigma L_x$ = total population (i.e., sum of all age groups) in a province, and
$N$ = number of provinces.

The weighted index of regional population inequality, $\Delta_w$, is

$$\Delta_w = \sum \frac{P}{\Sigma P} \left| \frac{L_x}{\Sigma L_x} - \frac{\sum \dfrac{L_x}{\Sigma L_x}}{N} \right|,$$

where   $P = \Sigma L_x$ = total population in a province, and
$\Sigma P$ = total population in Canada.

10 More precisely, the method of calculating $P$ is

$$P = \frac{\sum \left| \left( \dfrac{L}{P} \right)_i - \left( \dfrac{L}{P} \right) \right|}{N}$$

where   $\left( \dfrac{L}{P} \right)_i$ = labour force participation ratio of the $i$th region,

$\left( \dfrac{L}{P} \right)$ = labour force participation ratio for the nation as a whole, and

$N$ = total number of provinces.

For $P_w$ it is

$$P_w = \sum \left| \left( \frac{L}{P} \right)_i - \left( \frac{L}{P} \right) \right| \cdot \frac{f_i}{m},$$

where

$\left( \dfrac{L}{p} \right)_i$ and $\left( \dfrac{L}{P} \right)$ are the same as for $P$,

$f_i =$ total population in $i$th region, and

$m =$ national population.

11 The proof that these share differences represent a weighted deviation of the regional average income from the national level is as follows.

Let $\quad g_i =$ total output in the $i$th region,

$\quad\quad\;\; f_i =$ total population in the $i$th region,

$\quad\quad\;\; P =$ national output,

$\quad\quad\;\; n =$ national population.

Assume the *weighted share difference* for region $i$ is equal to the national average, then

$$\frac{g_i}{P} - \frac{f_i}{n} = 0, \text{ or} \tag{1}$$

$$\frac{g_i}{P} = \frac{f_i}{n}. \tag{2}$$

Again assume that the *weighted average deviation* for region $i$ is equal to the national average, then

$$\left( \frac{g_i}{f_i} - \frac{P}{n} \right) \frac{i}{n} = 0, \text{ and} \tag{3}$$

$$\frac{g_i}{n} = \frac{P.f_i}{n^2}, \tag{4}$$

$$\frac{g_i}{P} = \frac{f_i}{n} \tag{5}$$

Since (2) and (5) are identical, then the share differences represent the weighted deviations of provincial levels from the nation level, and

$$\sum \left| \frac{g_i}{P} - \frac{f_i}{n} \right| \quad \text{represents total regional inequality } (R_w).$$

12 This dual finding that regional inequality is an historical fact and that periods of divergence and convergence are witnessed was found in the United States. Measuring regional income in the U.S. back to 1840, it was found that inequality persisted from this early date to the present with a distinct widening in state per capita income differences between the middle and latter part of the nineteenth century; a decline in these differences, although not steady, through to 1950 was observed. Indeed, the differences among states in 1950 appear less than at any time in over a century. R. A. Easterlin, "Interregional Differences in Per Capita

Income, Population, and Total Income, 1840-1950," *Trends in the American Economy in the Nineteenth Century*, Studies in Income and Wealth, vol xxiv (Princeton, 1960), 73-140.

13 In his study of recent trends in regional income, Chernick concludes: "If it can be established that high levels of economic activity go hand in hand with its widespread regional diffusion, then the guidelines for a regional development policy might not be very different than those for national economic growth. If the contrary is true, it would imply that a high rate of national growth is not in itself a sufficient condition for securing an increased degree of regional participation. The data examined above, while far from conclusive, would tend to support the latter hypothesis, at least for the post-war period." S. E. Chernick, *Interregional Disparities in Income*, Staff Study 14, Economic Council of Canada (Ottawa, 1966), 65.

CHAPTER THREE

1 Denison calculates that only 0.05 percentage points of the growth rate of national product from 1929 to 1957 are attributable to a shift in the employment composition from farm to non-farm activities. Edward F. Denison, *The Sources of Economic Growth in the United States*, Supplementary Paper 13, Committee for Economic Development (1962), 227.

2 A widening in participation rates in the United States was observed between 1840 and 1880. Thereafter convergence occurred. Richard Easterlin, "Interregional Differences in Per Capita Income, Population, and Total Income, 1840-1950," *Trends in the American Economy in the Nineteenth Century*, Studies in Income and Wealth, vol xxiv (Princeton, 1960), 93-4.

3 The method of calculating the unweighted and weighted deviations and the relatives for GVA per worker is identical to that described for GVA per capita (Table III-2).

4 A similar divergence in per worker product was observed in the United States between 1840 and 1920. After 1920 convergence was observed. In fact for output per worker in the non-agricultural sector convergence was observed from 1840. *Ibid.*, 95.

CHAPTER FOUR

1 S. Kuznets, "Economic Growth and Income Inequality," *American Economic Review*, vol xlv (March 1955), 1-29. An application of this hypothesis to regional change in a number of countries has already been made. See Jeffrey G. Williamson, "Regional Inequality and the Process of National Development," *Economic Development and Cultural Change*, vol xiii (July 1965), part ii.

2 Kuznets, "Economic Growth and Income Inequality," 18.

3 Referring to developments since 1911, Easterbrook and Aitken say: "In the case of Canada, however, the development of industry has not supplanted older patterns

of staple production. Rather it has modified and supplemented them. Techno-
logical change has made possible the growth of an industrial sector in the Canadian
economy and has reduced Canada's previously extreme dependence on raw
material production." W. T. Easterbrook and H. G. J. Aitken, *Canadian Economic
History* (Toronto, 1956), 520.

4 Measured on a semi-log scale, homestead entries reached a peak by 1911. After
this date the rate of growth declines until the mid-1920s when a last "spurt" of
new settlement is observed. The latter terminates with the beginning of the 1930s.
Kenneth Buckley, *Capital Formation in Canada, 1896-1930* (Toronto, 1955), 14.

5 W. A. Mackintosh, *The Economic Background to Dominion-Provincial Relations*,
appendix III of the Royal Commission Report on Dominion-Provincial Relations,
reprinted in the Carleton Library Series (Toronto, 1964), 49-54.

6 It is interesting to note that changes in the sources of growth have not been
accompanied by any substantial "spread" of industrial structure among provinces.
The indexes of regional shares of mining and manufacturing (Table III-5), for
example, show levels in 1956 not very different from those of 1910. The implication is that in recent times labour (within Canada) has flowed towards capital
(industry) rather than capital to labour.

7 A revival of interest in the "staple theory" as one particular model of economic
growth is evident by the upsurge of recent writing on this topic. See, for example,
R. E. Caves and R. H. Holton, *The Canadian Economy* (Cambridge, Mass., 1961),
esp. ch. 2; R. E. Caves, " 'Vent for Surplus' Models of Trade and Growth," in
*Trade, Growth, and the Balance of Payments* (Chicago, 1966), 95-115; Douglass
C. North, "Location Theory and Regional Economic Growth," *Journal of Political
Economy*, vol LXII (June 1955), 243-58; Douglass C. North, *The Economic
Growth of the United States, 1790-1860* (Englewood Cliffs, N. J., 1961), esp.
ch. I; Melville H. Watkins, "A Staple Theory of Economic Growth," *Canadian
Journal of Economics and Political Science*, vol XXIX (May 1963), 141-58.

8 Since about the mid-1920s the share of agricultural products in total exports has
declined as has the share of total exports in Canada's GNP. See S. Kuznets, "Quantitative Aspects of the Economic Growth of Nations: x. Level and Structure of
Foreign Trade: Long Term Trends," *Economic Development and Cultural Change*,
vol 15, part II (January 1967), 116, 136.

APPENDIX B

1 For 1890 and 1910 the sectors estimated were agriculture, fishing and trapping,
forestry, mining, manufacturing, construction, transportation, personal and professional services, commerce, and government. For 1929 and 1956 all these sectors
were included plus utilities and finance.

2 O. J. Firestone, *Canada's Economic Development, 1867-1953*, Income and Wealth
Series VII (London, 1958), 282-97.

3 *Ibid.*, 285.

4 *Ibid.*, 289.

5 *Ibid.*, 292, for the calculation of this inflation index.

6 *Ibid.*, 289.

7 *Ibid.*, 291-2, for a complete description of how this figure was derived.

8 No explanation of how this figure was derived is given by Firestone.

9 The estimate of these percentages was from unpublished material of the DBS covering miscellaneous expenses of manufacturers in 1917 and 1920. *Ibid.*, 293.

10 *Ibid.*, 294, for details on how this figure was derived.

11 For a complete description of this procedure see appendix C.

12 Firestone gives a more complete description of this procedure. *Ibid.*, 265.

13 For a complete explanation of the method by which this redistribution was affected see appendix C.

14 For a list of sources see appendix C.

15 For a more complete statement of the possible biases involved in a single price deflator see S. Kuznets, *Modern Economic Growth* (New Haven, 1966), 94-6.

APPENDIX C

1 For an excellent study of the quality and consistency of long-term labour force estimates see F. T. Denton and Sylvia Ostry, *Historical Estimates of the Canadian Labour Force*, one of a series of labour force studies in the 1961 census monograph programme (Ottawa, 1967). The work outlined in this appendix was completed before publication of this monograph.

2 *Census of Canada, 1931*, vols VII and XII.

3 *Census of Canada, 1951*, vols IV and XI.

4 Decennial censuses provide the basic source of information for Tables C-1 to C-4. In particular, the *Census of Canada, 1951*, vol IV, Table 16, the *Census of Canada, 1931*, vol VII, Table 56, the *Census of Canada, 1911*, vol VI, Tables IV, V, and the *Census of Canada, 1891*, vol II, Table XII.

5 *Census of Canada, 1911*, vol VI, 48.

6 O. J. Firestone, *Canada's Economic Development, 1867-1953*, Income and Wealth Series VII (London, 1958), 281.

# INDEX

A sector (see also agriculture, fishing and trapping, forestry)
  provincial distribution: GVA 13, 15, 16, 56; labour force 16, 19, 55
  productivity: 59, 60
Agriculture 3, 16, 19, 20, 48, 54, 63, 65, 67; estimation of GVA 89-92
Alberta 2, 15, 19, 20; 1890-1910 63; 1910-56 39, 49, 59, 65, 67
Area 3

Bertram, G. W. 7n, 29
British Columbia 2, 8, 19, 20; 1890-1910 42, 49, 50, 55, 56, 63, 64, 67; 1910-56 39, 59, 65
British North America Act 1
Buckley, K. 63
Business cycle 23, 24

Canada 1, 8, 23, 25, 26, 41, 42, 50, 61, 66, 68
Canadian development 13, 23-4, 25, 26, 32, 33, 34, 45, 48, 64, 67, 68
Canadian economic history 68
Capital: foreign 66, 67
Caves, R. E. 24n, 66
Central provinces 64
Chernick, S. E. 42
Commodity 66
Construction: estimation procedure for GVA 95-6
Convergence: between provincial and national change 32, 33, 37; in terms of relative deviations from national level 49, 50, 54, 56; in relation to urban-industrial phase 65
Corporate profits 2n
Cost of living 3, 101

Daly, D. J. 25
Demand: income elasticity 45
Denison, E. F. 30n, 46
Denton, F. T. 102n
Depression 64
Determinants: regional growth 66, 68
Deviation: measure of 4, 41-2, 48-9, 51-2
Displacement index: calculation 30; and numerical results for gross value added 30, 32; for population 33, 35; for labour force 37, 39, 46
Divergence: absolute and relative deviations from national level 49, 51, 52, 54
Dominion of Canada 1

Easterbrook, W. T. 63n

Easterlin, R. A. 42n, 50n
Employment: indices of 16, 102
Exports 1, 67

Fishing and trapping: estimation procedure for GVA 92
Firestone, O. J. 29n, 84, 91, 103
Forestry: estimation procedure for GVA 93-4
Frontier settlement 24, 27; and spatial distribution 30, 32, 33, 35, 37, 45; and regional disparity 42, 48, 51, 68; and structural change 46, 54, 65; historical background 62-3, 66

Gross national product: United States 4, 25
Gross value added (output)
  rate of growth: total 3, 24-5, 30, 39, 42, 44; per capita 25, 26-7, 29, 64, 67; per worker 15, 28, 29-30
  spatial distribution: 30-2, 33, 37
  structure: share differentials 13-6, 19; changes in 45, 52, 56-7, 61, 63-4, 65
  estimation procedures: 84ff
  reconciliation: 99-100
  real: 101
Growth: national 23, 32, 65, 66, 67; regional 45, 52, 68

Howland, R. D. 2n, 11n

Immigration (see Migration)
Income
  definition: personal income 2, 3
  provincial differences per capita: personal 4; property 6; transfer 6, 7, 8; service 6, 9-13
  international differences: 1, 4, 15
Inequality: income 9; of participation rates 39-40; international 1
Internal migration (see Migration)
Inter- and intrasectoral inequality: calculation procedure 16, 19, 20, 46; results 19, 20, 22, 46, 48
Interwar period 37
Inverted U hypothesis 61-2, 64

Koffsky, N. 3
Kuznets, S. 4n, 15n, 16n, 19n, 24, 25, 29, 62, 67n

Labour force: definition 27, 102-3; participation rates 9, 27-8, 29, 30; growth of 28, 30; spatial distribution 10, 20, 37-9; age-sex composition 9, 11, 29, 30, 41;